All nature's works His praise declare, to whom they all belong;

There is a voice in every star, in every breeze a song.

Sweet music fills the world abroad with strains of love and power;

The stormy sea sings praise to God, the thunder and the shower.

Henry Ware

 Dedication

The Singing Silence (first edition), *The Winging Word*, *The Singing Silence* (second edition)

John Andrews
Belinda Cargill
James & Alison Collins
Edward I. Condren
Karen Cross
Alick Dowling
Piet & Beryll Geerlings
John & Johanna Geoghegan
Robin Giles
Amanda Greenslade

Bill Guttormsen
Jim & Dell Hamilton
Dale Harcombe
Peter Harris
Joan Helm
David Howlett
Lyn Hurry
Caroline Kettle
Andrew Lansdown
Gary Meisner
Steve McIntosh

Jonathan Olsen
Maree O'Hanlon
Shaun Pritchard
Rebekah Robinson
Mary Rofe
Natalie Schwarz
Pete Shayler-Webb
Robert D. Stevick
Bonnie Swain
Rose & Geoff Swete Kelly
and the folk at Tapanui

but most of all the anonymous author of *Pearl* and *Sir Gawain and the Green Knight* —a fourteenth century English poet for whom a new superlative is undoubtedly necessary. I used to think he was a genius, until I realised that was seriously underrating the depth of his talent. His unity of fine alliterative verse, theology, music, arithmetic, geometry, astronomy, history, geography, social commentary and the art of illumination is surely the single greatest artistic integration using the golden ratio of all time.

Contents

THE *Singing* SILENCE

Introduction

Back in 2003, I applied for several months of long service leave from a provincial high school, deciding at the last minute to spend my holiday teaching in central Australia. Every weekend while I was outback, I'd book a tour and head out to experience the sights. One Saturday, bumping along a red-dust road, it dawned on me that it was forty days since I'd arrived.

'Forty days in the desert!' I thought, remembering how significant that number was in various Scriptural stories about the wilderness. 'Perhaps God will have something special lined up for me today.' Consequently I was in a heightened state of expectancy as the mini-bus arrived at Rainbow Valley. The tour guide told us to be sure to be back by sundown to see the lights of sunset playing over the coloured rocks — but to explore as much as we liked until then. So I set out along a sandy trail towards Mushroom Rock, only to be surprised by a formation shaped like a crouching lion. I was lining it up for a photograph when I noticed a distant cliff-face with the profile of a man.

'Rainbow, lion, man,' I thought. My heart jolted as I recognised the symbolism. 'It's ok, it's ok.' I calmed my suddenly racing thoughts. 'There's no tree.' I realised that the combination of *rainbow, lion* and *man* was speaking to someone named Lewis. Only if a tree added to these emblems would it indicate there was a message in the landscape for someone named Hamilton.

The indigenous people of Australia talk about *songlines* or *dreaming tracks*. What I sensed was both incredibly similar and vastly different. The moment I saw Mushroom Rock — looking so much more like a tree than a fungus — I knew I had to consider the wild and scary possibility a message was encoded in the landscape for someone to collect. So I said to God: 'No doubt there have been lots of people named Hamilton pass this way, but probably none of them even remotely considered something as weird as asking to pick up a message hidden in the symbols of rock-shapes. And, Lord, I hate to mention this but I'm on a time budget. Like Cinderella's coach with its midnight deadline, my bus is leaving right after sunset. So, if I'm right, please be quick about teaching me to do this.'

He was quick. Just before sunset, I got the message. And it disconcerted me so much, I instinctively reacted by informing Him He had to tell someone else — not me! 'You can't expect me to do something about this! I'm a mathematics teacher!' As soon as I said that, I sighed with relief. 'Yes! I'm a mathematics teacher.' I calmed as I decided my profession let me off the hook. 'Tell You what, God. If You can explain this all to me in mathematics, I'll do it.' And I wiped my brow and thought: 'Phew! Close call. He'll never be able to do that.'

That, of course, is just about the most stupid thought ever. In retrospect I realise how naïve I was. Even some atheists recognise the universe has, as Stephen Hawking said, a mysterious 'fire in the equations'. As I came to understand that the design of the universe has its own message, it swiftly dawned on me I had to keep my promise to Him.

As a first step towards that, in 2007, the first edition of this book was published. It was small and slim and is now long out-of-print. This new edition combines the former text with fresh information. If you love mathematics, enjoy! And if you detest it, simply skip it. But either way, expect the unexpected.

Anne Hamilton
Seventeen Mile Rocks
Sukkot, September 2021

THE *Singing Silence*

Faith empowers us to see that the universe was created
and beautifully coordinated by the power of God's words!
He spoke and the invisible realm gave birth to all that is seen.
Hebrews 11:3 TPT

Amos 4:13 ISV
Look! The one who crafts mountains, who creates the wind,
who reveals what He is thinking to mankind, who darkens the morning light,
who tramples down the high places of the land—
the Lord, the God of the Heavenly Armies is His name.

THE *Singing Silence*

Where were you … when the morning stars sang together and all the Sons of God shouted for joy?

Job 38:4; 7 AMPC

Back in the 1960s, a group of geologists were exploring a strange circular bowl of mountains in Central Australia. The report of their findings[1] was startling: they concluded the ring formation was the eroded remains of an uplift caused by the impact of a comet or asteroid.

Soon specialists arrived to investigate the ancient crater. They were looking, amongst other things, for shattercones that display the distinctive 'horsetail' or 'angelhair' pattern only found when cosmic collisions have occurred. An astronomy magazine featured their work. When I read the description of the waveprints created at the very moment of impact and which were still visible in the rocks — *like a message*, the report said, *from the unimaginably distant past* — I determined I would go to the crater at Tnorala[2] one day.

What could possibly be so important, I wondered, *that God would crash a comet into outback Australia to write His message in rock?*

In retrospect, I didn't need to go there to find out. The epistle in the rock, the waveprint written in the shattercones at the time of

1.
One of the reasons the report was so startling was because, at the time, it was thought that meteoric impact craters were incredibly rare. Until the unmanned Soviet and American lunar expeditions of the late 1950s and early 1960s, even the craters on the moon were thought to be volcanic in origin. The prevailing opinion was that it was impossible for all meteors, asteroids or comets to come in at the same angle and hit the surface from directly overhead to form a perfect circle. So scientists considered that there should be many more teardrop and oval shapes. Eventually it was realised the speed of impact is so immense that the approach angle is comparatively insignificant.

2.
Tnorala is the name used by the Western Arrernte people. Maps also label it Gosses Bluff. The Dreaming associated with this formation tells of a group of starmaidens dancing across the sky. One of them, growing tired, placed a baby in a basket. It fell, plunging to earth. As it crashed, it overturned and hid the baby under the Bluff formed as the rocks were pushed up. It is remarkable, considering the estimated age of many outback craters, how many Dreaming stories involving cosmic impacts has been subsequently validated by science. One crater said to be millions of years old was actually found by astrophysicists after hearing traditional stories from Palm Valley about a star landing in Puka, the local waterhole.

impact, is also to be found in my garden, in every toothy smile that greets me, even in the shape of the credit card I use for shopping. God has written the same message all the way from the furthest corner of space to the microscopic fractal edges of a snowflake.

When we look up at the stars scattered across the night sky, we gaze back deep into the recesses of time. The light of the nearer stars has travelled just a few years to reach us. But the pinprick twinkles from the most distant of the observable galaxies have come from the dawn of the universe itself. They've not only journeyed across the vast reaches of space but also through long ages of time.

And yet — a great mystery is enfolded in these 'long ages of time'.

As far as the actual light itself is concerned, not a single minute has passed since it first set out. Not one! From our human point of view, locked as we are on a sea-wreathed planet slowly twirling across galactic space towards the solar apex, the starlight from the Pleiades has journeyed 444 years to reach us. But, if we could question a mote of light from that glowing blue star-cradle as soon as it reached

3.
According to Einstein's Theory of Relativity, as speed becomes faster and faster, time slows down. When an object reaches the speed of light (if it can, given other constraints), it cannot go any faster and time slows to zero. However, those watching the object will still find time passing because they are not travelling at this immense speed (equivalent to seven times around the earth in a second). For those of a technical mindset, elapsed time depends on both the speed of an object and the viewer's frame of reference with respect to that object.

5.
Louie Giglio overlays whalesongs and several different pulsars to produce the spectacular rhythm section of a cosmic symphonic orchestra, drumming out a harmonic beat in line with the great hymn, *How Great Is Our God.* (See youtube.com/watch?v=helxFeG-0n0). This book, *The Singing Silence*, examines God's mathematical signature rather than any musical one — though, of course, they are related.

us, it would report it had only just left. It would tell us that not even a single second had gone by since its departure. That no time has passed at all!

How do we wrap our thinking around this paradox? It seems so illogical.

Yet that's far from the case.[3] Time and eternity are entwined together so closely that, even as you read this, radio telescopes are picking up vibrations emanating from far beyond 444 light years. They are registering pulses right from the edge of the known universe — recording the voices of the morning stars as they sing their very first hymn of wonder. The *very first*. Right at this moment, the ancient throb of unimaginably distant pulsars is echoing across the Earth and sounding out the primal shout uttered so long ago by a joyful creation.

Yet what is the universe singing in this long morning[4] of creation? Is the song now just a jumble of static, its melody distorted by the stunningly huge distances it has travelled? Is it impossible to know what the Sons of God actually called out when they shouted for joy?

Or do we have a hope of comprehending the language of the stars and translating the lyrics of the angels' song of praise?

The heavens declare the glory of God; the skies proclaim the work of His hands. Day after day, they pour forth speech; night after night, they display knowledge.

Psalm 19:1–3[NIV]

I don't know the whole symphony of nature. But I do know that the chorus line, repeated by every creature nestled in the starlit curves of the universe, is not hard to find.[5] If we listen long enough to the voice of the silence, we will realise what it tells us about God and, through it, what God is telling us.

You shall also make a plate of pure *gold* and shall engrave on it, like the engravings of a seal: HOLY TO THE LORD.

Exodus 28: 36[NASB]

4.
The Hebrew word for *day* is 'yom', and is related to *sea*, 'yam'. In most languages, the word for *day* is in some way connected to *sunlight,* but not in Hebrew. Curiously, however, our technical words to describe the physics of light retain that connection to the sea: we have light *streams*, electromagnetic *waves*, electric *currents*. The implications of connecting a day as a measure of time to the movement of the sea are enormous. A marine current, for example, is a continuous directed movement of water within a wider body of ocean. Such currents facilitate faster movement of ships, just as jet streams in the atmosphere assist planes. If the word 'yom' for *day* has a similar connotation of internal currents then, long before Einstein discovered relativity, the Hebrew language always *implied* the concept. However, going beyond mere implication, there are *explicit* references to relativity in Scripture. 2 Peter 3:8 NIV quotes and augments Psalm 90:4 when it says, '*With the Lord a day is like a thousand years, and a thousand years are like a day.*' Peter gives us two conversion factors — and, using the relativistic equations of Einstein linking time and speed, it's not difficult to actually figure out the speed of the realm of heaven! This, according to my calculations for the first part of Peter's statement, is 0.99999999999625 of the speed of light or 299792457.9988 m/s. This is just 1.2 mm/s slower than the speed of light! Or, to put it another way, that distance of 1.2 mm is the same as the thickness of 22 pages of this book, while light can travel 7.48 times around the entire world in one second. But all this only holds true if we're talking about a 24-hour period, not daylight hours and Peter's words are ambiguous in that regard. If it is only daylight hours, then the distance the realm of heaven needs to speed up in order to reach the speed of light is the same as the thickness of 5 pages of this book in a total of 299792458 metres!

As a master craftsman finishes an article to his satisfaction, he stamps it with his personal mark. A potter impresses the clay, a silversmith etches the metal, a woodturner burns the surface and an artist signs the painting. The mark is usually discreet. Unlike a modern label worn blazoned on the front of a t-shirt, it's hidden away, unlikely to be noticed unless it's looked for. The mark is invariant — it doesn't change from one pot to the next, one painting to another, or from a silver candlestick to a silver spoon.

Now the master craftsman of the entire cosmos[6] is God. From the glittering sweep of the furthest galaxy to deep within the chromosomal heart of the double helix, all of creation is God's handiwork. It is His tour de force of perfect design and, with it, He pronounced Himself well-pleased.

And God saw everything that He had made and, behold, it was very good.

Genesis 1:31[RSV]

He is the consummate craftsman. So, does it sound irreverent to suggest that, like a human artisan, God has signed all of His work? Perhaps it seems a little impertinent to propose that the Maker of the universe has an invariant hallmark He has stamped on every work of His hands from stars to people, daisies to comets, shells to bananas, parrots to sheep, hurricanes to butterflies, snowflakes to beehives, dandelions to apples, feathers to claws.

Perhaps this sounds like anthropomorphising God, making Him in man's image. On the other hand, perhaps we feel a need to sign our work because, in doing so, we reflect an aspect of God as creator.

Where would we look for a hidden mark? Well, if it really is everywhere, then it shouldn't particularly matter. If

6.
Some medieval poets, knowing that 'cosmos' means *ornament*, conceived of a beautiful image— God wearing His entire creation as a dazzling jewelled brooch, close to His heart.

God has a special seal He has stamped on everything, then it shouldn't make any difference where we choose to start. The puzzle might occasionally be slightly difficult because ours in a fallen world. However, even if the mark is marred, it should still be recognisable as an ideal form.

One of the greatest riddles in genetics is found in the hive of the velvet-bodied bumble-bee. Most animals of more than a single cell have both a mother and a father. Not so bees. Sexual reproduction for them is so different that is has a special name: haploid. The female workers are the result of a classic two-parent union; they are descended from both a mother and a father. The male drones, on the other hand, are not. They have no father, only a mother: the queen.

Consequently, an imbalance of genders is present in the hive. There are far more females than there are males.[7] In an exemplary, well-established hive the ratio of males to females is 0.618 to 1. Curiously, this same number is found in sunflowers. If you compare two interesting seed spirals in the head of a sunflower, you'll find that the ratio of one to the other tends toward 0.618 to 1 as the flower gets bigger. The same is true for the intersecting bracts of a pineapple, the scales of a pinecone or the florets of a broccoli. A dandelion, a red clover flower, a thistle, breadfruit, cauliflower, Queen Anne's Lace, and the spiky seedpods of the golden allamander also show similar intersecting spirals. Mathematically, these are all related to the equiangular spiral, a shape that can be constructed from a succession of squares built on a rectangle whose sides are in the ratio of 0.618 to 1.

Ever since the creation of the world, God's invisible qualities—God's eternal power and divine nature—have been clearly seen, because they are understood through the things God has made.

Romans 1:20[CEB]

Curves of this type can be found in an extraordinarily diverse number of places: the coiled tails of the chameleon and the seahorse, the spiral of a whirlwind seen from space, the unfolding fiddlehead of a new fern leaf, the cross-section of a nautilus or a fossil ammonite, the tail feathers of a lyrebird, the twisting crowns of trees in a eucalypt forest, the pearlescent architecture inside the abalone or the paua, the spiral mark on the 'door' of a cat's eye shell, the curl of a ram's horn shell and even the ringed horns of the mouflon ram after which the shell is named. Parts—or segments—of the curve are also common: they're found in comet's tails, elephants' tusks, dolphins' fins, birds' beaks, cats' claws, the curvature of feathers and the shape of bananas. The answer to that hoary old question 'Why is a banana bent?' is simple: if it were straight, it wouldn't bear God's hallmark.

Once the spiral is drawn out of the two dimensional plane into three dimensions, then an enormous vista opens up: amongst the shells alone, there are turrets, turbans, trumpets, tops, trophons, corkscrews, casks, periwinkles, pagodas, mitres, sundials, violets, whelks, wentletraps, neritas, helmets and volutes, not to mention the ordinary snail. And this is to name only a few local South Pacific types.

There are three things too wonderful for me to understand— no, four! Firstly, how an eagle glides through the sky...

Proverbs 30:18–19TLB

The gyre of a hawk, a falcon or an eagle is a remarkable example of this spiral. A bird of prey keeps one eye constantly directed towards its target as it circles ever closer before making a sudden plummet. To achieve such a focussed gaze, the path such a bird traces out is an equiangular spiral—this very same spiral that is built on a rectangle whose sides are in the ratio 0.618 to 1.

The division of a plant stem into branches often follows closely this same spiral path. However it doesn't have to be a spiral to conform to this proportion. Limpets, in their asymmetry, show a ratio tending towards 0.618 to 1. Maple leaves also highlight 0.618 to 1 in their design. The iridescent eyes of peacock feathers are positioned in the same proportion; so are the bandings on fish, the markings on butterflies, the petal arrangement of white-spoked daisies, and the dark Cassini Division in the rings of the planet Saturn. The ratio is found in sunspot cycles; in the rhythmic drumming of the pulsar at the centre of the Crab Nebula; in the transition from Newtonian mechanics to Einstein's relativistic physics; in fact, so it's reported, in the very shape of the universe itself.

A rose is arranged in envelopes of petals which increasingly tend towards this ratio. Celery and leeks have stems which interleave one another in the same numerical pattern. Black and white stripes on a zebra aren't the same size but have the same relationship as your front tooth to the one next to it. The proportion of the length to the width of a human chromosome is close to this ratio as well.

> **So God created man in His own image,**
> **in the image of God He created him.**
>
> Genesis 1:27–28[KJV]

Half a millennium ago it was common knowledge that this proportion was the fundamental basis of God's design. It was acknowledged as His signature across all of creation. It's not just found in nature; it's found within Scripture itself, especially—of course—throughout the first chapter of Genesis. How could it be otherwise? How could anyone properly describe the days of creation without noting the mathematical principle used to hallmark it all?

8.
I am using Jewish spelling here; for most people this will only be noticeable in the use of 'elokim' instead of 'elohim'.

9.
For some Jewish scholars, there is significance in the word *alef-tav* preceding the creation of either heavens or earth in the Genesis record. It becomes therefore the vessel of creation, giving shape and substance to creation. It is also the method of creation, as well as the twofold witness to creation; and, besides formatting creation, *alef-tav* also encodes meaning into it. See, for example, David Patterson, *Hebrew Language and Jewish Thought*, Routledge 2009

10.
See, for example, Anne Hamilton, *God's Panoply: The Armour of God and the Kiss of Heaven*, Armour Books 2016, or for data analysing the mathematics of John's Gospel, see M.J.J. Menken, *Numerical Literary Techniques in John: The Fourth Evangelist's Use of Numbers of Words and Syllables* (Novum Testamentum, Supplements) 1985

בראשית ברא אלהים **את** השמים ואת הארץ

(G)   (F)   (E)   (D)   (C)   (B)   (A)

bereshit (A)

bara (B)

Elokim[8] (C)

et (D)

hashamaim (E)

v'et (F)

haarets (G)

These first seven words open the book of Genesis and describe the creation of the heavens and the earth, a wondrous accomplishment that came about through the breath of God.

**By the word of the Lord the heavens were made,
their starry host by the breath of His mouth.**

Psalm 33:6[NIV]

God spoke His treasure—the glittering, jewelled cosmos—into being. Jewish scholars suggest He created the universe using the letters of the alphabet. The word emphasised in bold above in the Hebrew of Genesis 1:1 is *alef-tav*: *alef* is the first letter of the Hebrew alphabet and *tav* is the last letter. It is untranslated in English versions of the Bible. Many Christian scholars consider alef-tav as simply a grammatical pointer; however, Jewish writers see it as representing the alphabet and all possible word combinations of it.[9]

Yet, because letters and numbers are not separate in Hebrew, rich mathematical relationships exist within these words. Using the value assigned to each letter, we can calculate the numerical value of each of the first seven words:

(A) bereshit = 913

(B) bara = 203

(C) elokim = 86

(D) et = 401

(E) hashamayim = 395

(F) v'et = 407

(G) haarets = 296

$A+C = 913+86 = 999$

$B+D+E = 203+401+395 = 999$

$C+E+F = 86+395+407 = 888$

$A+B+C+D+E = 1998 = 2 \times 999$

These are multiples of 111, a number signifying *covenant*.[10]

$B+G = 499$

$D+F = 808$

$^{499}/_{808} = 0.618$

$^{808}/_{1307} = 0.618$ — where $1307 = B+D+F+G$

Now perhaps you have recognised 0.618 as the 'golden ratio'.[11] Long before its modern renaming, it was called the 'Divine Proportion'. Way back in the first century, it was inestimably revered by the Greeks as the building block of formal beauty and elegance across architecture, sculpture, art and even works of literature. Every ratio[12] was termed 'logos' by the Greeks, but when they referred to '**the** logos', they meant this lovely mathematical structure found throughout nature that was so pleasing to the eye.

Now, if, by this time, you'd reached the conclusion that the golden ratio is to be found in John 1:1 as well as Genesis 1:1, you'd be right.

Are you wondering how we've forgotten all this? Are you curious as to why we no longer know what our ancestors took for granted?

Now perhaps you have recognised the golden ratio because, for a while, it was part of a cultural phenomenon. In the first decade of this century it rose to prominence through Dan Brown's bestseller, *The Da Vinci Code*. In his blockbuster Brown claimed the golden ratio has always been a symbol of goddess worship. He suggested Leonardo da Vinci's fascination with it stemmed from his involvement in a heretical and hidden religious cult.

The idea makes for a fast-moving adventure-mystery but the actual facts are quite ordinary. A certain mathematically-minded friar, Luca Pacioli, had written a treatise on the golden ratio. He called his manuscript '*The Divine Proportion*'. Now, unless you're an accountant, you've probably never heard of Pacioli. All he's remembered for today is introducing double-entry book-keeping to the world. But he wasn't unknown or obscure back in the early sixteenth century. In fact he was not only exceedingly well-known but he had sufficient clout to be able to choose his own manuscript illustrator. So he appointed an up-and-coming artist from the town of Vinci named Leonardo.

Pacioli was captivated by the 'Divine Proportion'[13] and was able to enthuse Leonardo with his passion. He found five attributes of God hidden in it. The first was Unity and the second Trinity.

He believed that a clue was encoded in this very special numerical ratio and that it pointed to the three-in-one, one-in-three nature of God. Pacioli is considered to have 'rediscovered' a lost understanding of the golden ratio known since the sixth century *before* Christ. The Greek mathematician Pythagoras is often credited with having first devised the theorem to explain it. However, it's unlikely he was the discoverer. It's almost certain that he gained his knowledge during the time he spent with the magi of Babylon.[14]

It is Pythagoras, not Pacioli, whose influence on the understanding of the golden ratio has passed down to modern times in two principal forms:

- the first, mathematical
- the second, magical

Pacioli's influence is often considered to be vastly less than that of Pythagoras because, as is often pointed out, he gave no practical advice to artists on how to apply the 'divine proportion' to their endeavours.[15] But that is to ignore the successful burial of God's connection with the golden ratio in the nineteenth century. Before that, it was widely recognised.

Long before Pacioli wrote his famous treatise, English poets routinely made use of the divine proportion to create an internal architecture for their illuminated poetry.[16] One of the greatest—and surely the most underrated—Christian works of fiction is the *Pearl* manuscript, a series of four brilliant poems including *Sir Gawain and the Green Knight*. These fourteenth century poems are designed as a unity, using the golden ratio in their mathematical substructure to underscore the hidden aspects of God in creation, as well as His work of salvation in Jesus.[17]

Creativity in medieval times was entirely different from our own contemporary ideas. Artists and poets, sculptors and jewellers, city-planners and composers looked to Scripture for inspiration and re-interpreted the mathematics they found there in their own work. That was how they thought of 'creativity'.[18]

15.
There are two answers to this criticism. First, there was really no need for him to give any practical tips. He was very likely advancing the theory behind an extremely common practice. His work is basically a translation of a treatise by the renowned Renaissance artist, Piero della Francesca. Secondly, just as Pacioli failed to credit della Francesca, his own contribution was deliberately concealed in the early twentieth century. Theodore Andrea Cook in the influential *The Curves of Life*, an examination of biological growth published in 1912, quoted many examples from the work of Leonardo but never mentioned the term 'Divine Proportion.' The name *phi* was advocated by Cook's colleague, William Schooling, who promoted the idea of American mathematician Mark Barr. Schooling waxed exuberant about the 'discovery' of *phi*—never once suggesting that it was a repackage of an antique concept or mentioning any of its older names except 'golden section', a name used in Germany for less than a century. John Leslie is quoted but his term, 'medial section', is not. Leonardo is lionised but neither 'sectio aurea' nor 'divina proportione' are mentioned. *The Curves of Life* ultimately comes across as a deliberate attempt to occlude God and promote humanism. The name 'phi' comes from Phidias, who rebuilt the Parthenon. Many people think that 'phi' and the golden ratio are the same, but 'phi' is actually a growth factor of approximately 1.618 while the golden ratio is rounded to 0.618. One is the inverse proportion of the other.

16.
See, for example, Thomas Elwood Hart, *Medieval Structuralism: Dulcarnoun and the Five-Book Design of Chaucer's Troilus*, jstor.org/stable/25093786 (accessed 19 July 2020); Robert David Stevick, *The Earliest Irish and English Bookarts: Visual and Poetic Forms Before 1000 A.D.*, University of Pennsylvania Press 1994; Edward I. Condren, *The Numerical Universe of the Gawain-Pearl Poet—Beyond Phi*, University Press of Florida 2002; Joan Helm abc.net.au/radionational/programs/scienceshow/science-mathematics-and-the-riddles-of-camelot/3361664 (accessed 19 July 2020).

17.
Anne Hamilton, *Gawain and the Four Daughters of God: The Testimony of Mathematics in Cotton Nero A.x*, Armour Books 2014

This resulted in intricate and complicated verses that break all the more modern ideas of regular length. Some English poets were Christian and designed their 'poetic architecture' based on the golden ratio as it was found in Scripture. Others followed the lead of French writers who were using Pythagorean mysticism and magic.

Whatever philosophy the authors followed, Biblical or Pythagorean, they could all agree that nature displayed the golden ratio everywhere anyone looked!

As society changed in medieval Europe, the realisation that God had signed His handiwork, both in Scripture and in creation, came under threat. The troubadours who introduced the idea of 'courtly love' to Europe sometimes used the golden ratio as an accompaniment to the symbol of 'woman as goddess'. A modern update on this idea is, in fact, *The Da Vinci Code*. Same ideology, different century.

Strangely, the troubadours used Pythagorean mathematics while totally ignoring one of its central tenets — the feminine principle is evil. It's the fusion of this Greek philosophic idea with Scriptural interpretation that has resulted in the centuries-long devaluation of women, a devaluation largely absent in Scripture itself.[19]

Now in one of the most famous of all manuscripts — *Le Chevalier de la Charette*, a story that introduces Sir Lancelot of the Lake to the legends of King Arthur and the Round Table — a mysterious illuminated E is found at the golden ratio position in the text. Almost certainly, this alludes to the famous and enigmatic E inscribed on the navelstone in the temple of Python Apollo at Delphi in Greece. (And yes, if you suspected a relationship between the names Pythagoras and Python Apollo, you'd be right. The philosopher was named after the godling.)

The shrine of Python Apollo was made famous by the Delphic Oracle, a priestess who, in a trance, answered questions in a strange, heavenly tongue. These perplexing replies were regarded as prophetic utterances and were interpreted by the attendant priests.

Now Python Apollo is referred to in Scripture: once very directly[20] and at least one other time very subtly and obliquely.[21] Both occasions were in connection with the Apostle Paul.

18.
Robert Stevick, for example, has brilliantly demonstrated the processes by which Anglo-Saxon poetry, Celtic illuminated manuscripts such as the *Book of Kells* and the *Book of Durrow*, as well as ivory carvings, stone crosses, leather book covers and ornaments such as the Hunterston Brooch were embellished by designs based on the golden ratio.

19.
I recognise that a statement like this will seem outrageously impossible to some people. See, however, how significant the role of women in Scripture really is, as pointed out in: *More Precious than Pearls* (2016), and its sequels, *As Resplendent as Rubies* (2020) and *As Exceptional as Sapphires* (2021): *The Mother's Blessing and God's Favour Towards Women I, II, III*, Armour Books.

20.
'One day, as we were going to the house of prayer, we encountered a young slave girl who had an evil spirit of divination, the spirit of Python. She had earned great profits for her owners by being a fortune-teller.' Acts 16:16 TPT

21.
1 Corinthians 13:1–13

The temple of Apollo at Delphi sat high on cliffs overlooking the Bay of Corinth. Seekers came there from all over the ancient world, looking for answers to difficult questions. They would come to the priestess who sat, chewing laurel leaves, breathing noxious fumes, and waiting to utter her riddling prophecies in a strange, babbling language. Croesus, a king proverbial for his wealth, came to inquire about the outcome of a campaign he was considering—and then famously failed to recognise the ambiguity of the answer. *If Croesus invades*, said the oracle, *a great empire will be destroyed.* But she didn't say which empire.

Humbler men came asking advice about possible trade ventures, likely marriage partners, suitable crops to plant and the best time to plant them. Nero came and asked what the E on the navelstone meant.

Plutarch, who was later to become the high priest at Delphi, discussed Nero's question with friends. His two best guesses were that the E was an ancient Greek formulation for 'if' or alternatively 'I am'. He pointed out that questions to the sibyl often began with 'if'. Her answers also often began with 'if'.

If...   I am...

Words that open the door on the question of freewill. The *Pearl* poet of the fourteenth century connected the operation of freewill choices with the golden ratio. Strangely enough, it would be the twentieth century before that particular link would pop up again—and it wouldn't be in poetry, but in business and the stock market.[22]

Still, back in the fourteenth century when the universe and everything in it was routinely understood to be God's, both poetry and the building of cathedrals were based around designs using the golden ratio. Cathedrals in France used it in the architecture. It wasn't a new idea. It's integral to the shape of a number of free standing crosses in Ireland. Around the ninth century, Cynewulf used it to create *Elene,* a poem featuring the True Cross. In the seventh century, Eadfrith had used the golden ratio as an integral part of the design of the Lindisfarne gospel. It was commonly used in illuminated manuscripts, particularly those executed in the distinctively Celtic manner.

So it wasn't a revolution when Leonardo de Vinci started to use it. The best artists of the west had known about it for *at least* three quarters of a millennium when he breathed new life into it—and architects had known about it a lot longer.

In fact the golden ratio had been around so long it isn't surprising Luca Pacioli dealt with it at a more theoretical level. His treatise,

22.
Elliott Wave Theory is the present-day study of fluctuations in the stock market. Its wider implications have been recognised as involving the mathematical relationship between choice and chance, or freewill and fate.

23.
It's certainly close, but it's rarely perfect. I incline to the suspicion that Pacioli was influenced by the medieval notion (held by neo-Platonists of the era) that the golden ratio was linked to their alleged navelstone of the world at the temple of Python Apollo in Delphi. See Anne Hamilton, *Gawain and the Four Daughters of God: The Testimony of Mathematics in Cotton Nero A.x*, Armour Books 2014

24.
Through the examination of successively smaller golden ratio segments, Pacioli and Leonardo noted the positioning of the elbow, the length of the forearm, the distance from the crown to the inside top of the arm, the size of the head and so on. Yet despite the extensive catalogue of relationships that Pacioli found and that Leonardo drew, they by no means exhausted the ways human beings show the 'divine proportion'.

The Divine Proportion, is more of a commentary than a practical guide. He did make a great contribution, however, through his sense of wonder and enthusiasm, an enthusiasm for precise mathematics which he passed on to his artistic friends. Leonardo's pictures analyse the human body and, in the successive divisions of the face and torso, reveal the 'divine proportion'.

Leonardo wasn't the only artist influenced and mentored by Pacioli. So was the German artist, Albrecht Dürer. Pacioli believed the ideal individual had his navel at the golden ratio of his height.[23] Both Leonardo and Dürer have left fine sketches showing this design — Leonardo's being the famous *Vitruvian Man.* Both artists also saw this same distance in a measurement from the top of the head to the fingertips. Leonardo also noticed that finger joints occur in relation to each other close to the divine proportion and also realised that the length of the forearm compared to the hand was basically 0.618 to 1. He drew pictures in which the eyes are positioned midway in a golden rectangle enclosing the head, and the mouth and nose are shown to be at the two golden sections which lie between the eyes and the chin. He sketched the curve of the ear as part of an equiangular spiral, and showed that the opening of the ear is at a golden ratio position from the front to the back of the head.[24]

For You created my inmost being; You knit me together in my mother's womb.
I praise You because I am fearfully and wonderfully made;
Your works are wonderful, I know that full well.

Psalm 139:13–14[NIV]

The Divine Proportion is found in the curled form of the foetus inside the mother's womb, the whorl of hair at the crown of the head, the coil of the Eustachian tubes inside the ear, the dimensions of chromosomes inside the double helix of DNA, the relationship between the width of one tooth and the next — even in a human heartbeat. Most mysteriously of all, if the observations in *New Scientist* are correct, then it is present in the deep workings of the human mind. In a 2002 article,[25] it was reported that decision-making in human beings is neither as free nor as rational as we would like to think and that we live our lives according to particular numeric patterns of which we are not conscious.

What number dominates those numeric patterns? It appears those fourteenth century English poets were right. Freewill and the golden ratio really are inextricably linked.

Clearly God has an inordinate fondness for this particular number. So it should come as no surprise to find the instructions He gave Noah for building the ark incorporate it. The extra height God instructs Noah to factor in for the windows, just below the roof, creates a dimension which is very close to the golden ratio to the width.

'Very close' obviously wasn't good enough, however, when it later came to another construction. Solomon's Temple had an exact golden ratio dimension built into the entrance to the inner sanctuary. 1 Kings 6:31 tells us that, while the outer openings had four sides, the doorway to the inner sanctum was a pentagon, a shape that has the golden ratio built into the intersection of its diagonals.

Here it's worthwhile pausing a moment to reflect.

The earth is the Lord's, and everything in it, the world, and all who live in it.

Psalm 24:1[NIV]

If we truly believe that the earth and its fullness belong to God, we won't wrongly attribute ownership of the most spiritually controversial of all signs and symbols: the five-pointed star — known to mathematics as the pentagram.

It is a little over a hundred years since the pentagram became almost exclusively associated with black magic. Abandoned by modern-day Christians and left to the adherents of New Age religion and to devotees of witchcraft, the pentagram is often viewed by Christians with suspicion. It is almost incomprehensible that, like the fish and the anchor, the pentagram was reputedly a first century symbol of Jesus.

It was also at one time a symbol of Jerusalem, as well as the emblem adopted by the Pythagorean Brotherhood as their device of mutual recognition. They called it "man's number" or "the number of man".

This calls for wisdom. If anyone has insight, let him calculate the number of the beast, for it is man's number. His number is 666.

Revelation 13:18[NIV]

Almost universally overlooked in the search to identify the Anti-Christ, Pythagoras (whose name adds in one numerological system to 666 and in another to 216 — 6x6x6 — and whose Brotherhood had as their emblem 'man's number') may well have been understood by early Christianity as the ultimate usurper.[26] Pythagorean mysticism had infiltrated early Christianity via the Gnostics. The Apostle John is said, on discovering a well-known Gnostic was in the baths he was about to enter, to have grabbed his clothes and left hastily in case God's judgment was about to descent. The mark of the beast, being also the 'number of man', is probably the pentagram. To complicate matters, the 'cross' in the following passage may also actually be a pentagram.

He called the man in white with a scribe's inkhorn in his belt and said, "Go all through the city, all through Jerusalem, and mark a cross on the foreheads of all who deplore and disapprove of all the filth practiced in it."

Ezekiel 9:3b–4 (Jerusalem Bible)

The cross or mark mentioned here, the 'taw' in the original, was understood by Francis of Assisi as a reference to the tau cross, the t-shape he favoured rather than our modern Latin cross. 'Tau' was one of the names for the golden ratio before the twentieth century when it became associated with the name 'phi' (which is approximately 1.618 rather than 0.618).

Is it baffling that the Mark of the Beast is almost certainly the same as the mark of God's chosen remnant? Why should we be surprised? Satan doesn't have an original idea—he's a thief, not a creator.

25.
John Casti, *"I know what you'll do next summer"*, New Scientist, 31 August 2002. newscientist.com/article/mg17523585-500-i-know-what-youll-do-next-summer/ (accessed 19 July 2020)

26.
Pythagoras lived in the sixth century B.C. but the major stories of his life date from the second century A.D. 800 years lie between his life and the major records of it, though fragmentary earlier tales have been passed down. He is said not to have been referred to by name; but like the ineffable word Yahweh, his was not to be spoken, so his devotees referred to 'HIM'. There is a marked resemblance to Jesus' miracles and Pythagoras' feats of magic, including a 'resurrection' after three years of 'burial' underground, as well as a marvellous draught of fishes. The repeated use of the number 17 to structure both the gospels and epistles suggests major opposition to the infiltration of Pythagorean theurgy into early Christianity. For more on this, as well as the possible relationship between the Pythagorean Brotherhood and 666, see Anne Hamilton, *Dealing with Leviathan: Spirit of Retaliation*, Armour Books 2020.

Even in the deepest, darkest magic, there remains an implicit understanding the pentagram really does belong to God. His sovereignty is inferred all through the classic tales where a sorcerer chalks two pentagrams on the floor, one to protect himself, the other to bind the demon he calls up. If there is a protective symbol that can control any demon, then logically the power behind that symbol must be more powerful than any demon. Only God has power that comprehensive.

Since Christians have wiped their hands of this symbol, everyone seems to want it. Freemasons have a long association with the golden ratio while twenty-first century proponents of goddess worship also claim these aspects of the pentagram as their own. They point to the fact that, if you slice an apple crossways, you'll find a five-pointed star hidden at the centre of the fruit. Thus they claim both apple and star as an emblem of the goddess.

The apple isn't the only place the pentagram is found in nature. Like the spiral, its diversity is immense. It's found in the cross-section of a pear as well as a papaya, in the shape of a dog rose, blue borage, waxy orange blossom and the frangipani to name but a few of a staggering number of five-petalled flowers. In the sea, it's found in starfish and all the curious varieties of sand dollars. In the heavens, it's found in the orbit of our nearest planetary neighbour. When viewed from Earth, successive inferior conjunctions of Venus trace out an almost perfect pentagram around the sun every eight years.

The golden ratio is inescapably and repeatedly present in the pentagram. In one sense, since smaller pentagrams can be successively drawn inside larger ones, it's present in an infinite number of ways.

The pentagram can be viewed two ways. Because it can be drawn without lifting pen from paper, it is sometimes called the 'Endless Knot.' The other way of looking at it is as three overlapping triangles. As the Endless Knot, the lines intersect each other at the golden ratio position. The length Y is 0.618 of the line X. The length X is 0.618 of Z, which is 0.618 of the whole line.[27]

0.618 to 1 equals 1 to 1.618 and also equals[28] 1.618 to 2.618. Now normally when you divide into 1, you wind up with different digits

27.
There are many other golden ratio aspects in this diagram — in fact, if we were to draw a pentagram within the central pentagon and then another within its central pentagon, we would quickly realise there an infinite number of golden ratio features.

28.
Please remember these numbers are always rounded. Even the number in the next paragraph, 0.618033988749 89484820458683436564, is rounded off from an infinite, non-repeating decimal. If you want accuracy, it's $0.5 \times \sqrt{5} - 0.5$ you're looking for.

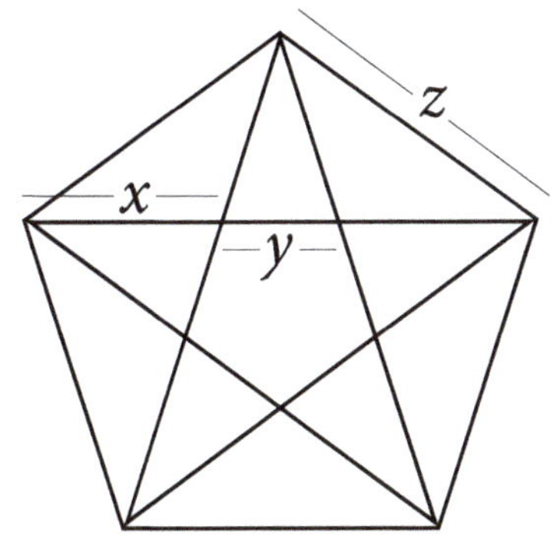

than the ones you started with. For example when you divide 1 by 2 you wind up with a 5 in the decimal 0.5 and when you divide 3 by 4 you wind up with a 7 and a 5 in the number 0.75.

The only number you can divide into 1 and wind up with the same digits you started with is—

$$0.6180339887498948482045868343656 4...$$

Try it on a calculator putting in as many decimals as your calculator will hold:

1 divided by 0.618... = 1.618...
And 1.618... divided by 0.618 ... = 2.618...
There it stops: you won't be able to add one more by dividing by 0.618...
What this very special set of operations additionally means is this:

$$0.618 \text{ to } \mathbf{1} \ = \ \mathbf{1} \text{ to } 1.618 \ = \ 1.618 \text{ to } \mathbf{1} + 1.618$$

Look at them again closely: there are three equal relationships involving the number 1. Hold that thought: three equal relationships involving the number 1 that happen to be found almost anywhere you look in the universe. *Unity*, Pacioli said. *Trinity*.

Hold that thought steady indeed while we go back to the pentagram and look at it as a triple triangle.

The three triangles which made up the pentagram are identical. Each has, as all plane triangles do, 180° as the total sum of its angles. This means that the total of the angles of all three triangles is 540°, which happens to be the same number of degrees as the central pentagon. Each of the three triangles is what is called an isosceles triangle—that means two of its sides are equal in length and so are two of its angles. As it transpires, the largest angle is 108° and the smaller angles are 36° each. This means that the larger angle is three times the smaller ones.

Think of it as three triangles in each of which one angle is three times the others and which as a totality can collapse into the single central form, which can then enclose another three triangles in each of which one angle is three times the others and which as a totality can collapse into the single central form—and so on to infinity.

Three in one, one in three.

If we go back to the Endless Knot, we realise that the three-in-one, one-in-three, is an equal *relationship*. The digits are the same but the numbers are different — and it is the *relationships*, not the numbers, which are *equal*.

There aren't too many equations that leave mathematicians at a loss for words. Formulae which are stumblingly described as 'beautiful' or 'superbly elegant' are quite rare.[29] If I'm not quite articulate here, I'm in good company. Jakob Bernoulli, a seventeenth century scientist who examined the logarithmic spiral, took one look at the curious invariant equality of the mathematics describing it under all sorts of transformations and immediately thought of rebirth and resurrection. '*Although changed, I rise again the same*' is what he wanted on his gravestone, along with the spiral[30] itself. Resurrection is not the thought that automatically occurs to me when equal relationships are involved, exquisite as Bernoulli's idea is. The first analogy I think of outside of mathematics when the notion of equal relationships is broached is simply 'love'.

Love.

Encoded in the mathematics of the universe[31] is this message over and over and over again: God is a *Trinity and, because of the equal relationships, God is love.*

Patrick, patron saint of Ireland, held up a shamrock to demonstrate Trinity to the druids. It's a terrific symbol, too, because, like every other created thing, it hides the golden ratio in its form and whispers God's ineffably wonderful secret: He is Trinity and He is love.

That's why 0.618 is locked into human freewill. Only when this number is factored into our decision-making do we reflect God.

29.
E = mc2 doesn't even make it to the Top 10 Awesome Equations. Apparently it's $e^{i\pi} + 1 = 0$ that causes dewy-eyed sighs in the greatest number of scientists and mathematicians. If you happen to have enough background to appreciate that equation, check out youtube.com/watch?v=Ka2Y86JTZ58 which demonstrates John 1:1 contains a very close approximation of the natural logarithm, e. Once you recover from that mind-blowing experience, try otherbiblecode.com/Pi_File.htm, which reveals there's an extremely accurate value of π encoded in Genesis 1:1. On a tangentially related front, the whole numbers 3 and 7 can be created using the golden ratio and the inverse square rule. Start with the exact value of the golden ratio ($0.5 \times \sqrt{5} - 0.5$) and find its inverse square; then add to that answer the square of the golden ratio. That's how you get *exactly* 3 from an *irrational* number! For 7, start again with the exact value of the golden, then find the square of its inverse square; to that, add the square of the square of the golden ratio.

30.
Unfortunately for Bernoulli, the stonecutter didn't realise there are different spirals, so he carved an Archimedean rather than a logarithmic one.

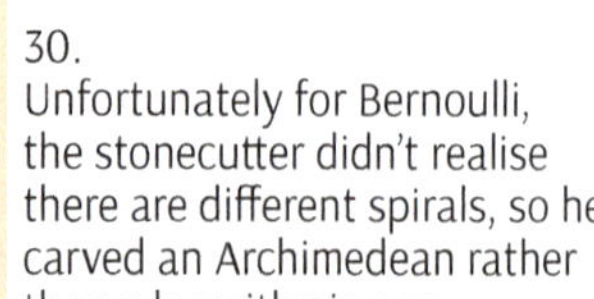

But, having said that, *how* do we factor 0.618 into our decisions? I'm going to take a medieval clue linking 0.618 to the navelstone of Delphi as well as to a letter from Paul of Tarsus to the people living in the town across the bay from the famous oracle. Paul's words take that mysterious 'if' and connect it straight back to the essence, not just of who God is, but also who we are and how we should make decisions.

> ***If*** **I speak in the tongues of men and of angels,**
> **but have not <u>*love*</u>,**
> **<u>I am</u> a noisy gong or a clanging cymbal.**
> **And *if* I have prophetic powers,**
> **and understand all mysteries and all knowledge,**
> **and *if* I have all faith so as to remove mountains,**
> **but have not <u>*love*</u> <u>I am</u> nothing.**
>
> 1 Corinthians 13:1–2[RSV][32]

We're not star-stuff, despite what Carl Sagan famously said. As Francis of Assisi rightly observed, it's *brother* sun and *sister* moon. We're not descended from the stars, we're their siblings. Like them, we're designed with a hidden hallmark. And yet, it's not just in the disciplined arrangement of galaxies and the careful order of orbiting planets that God's signature mark is found. Deep within chaos, within the fractal patterns at the heart of disorder —the golden ratio is there too. Wherever we look in the universe, there is a silent testimony that God is a trinity and God is love.

In our daily lives, God requires that we love Him and love our neighbour. Everything in the universe has this tell-tale ratio and is designed to remind us about the two great commandments. Unless each choice, each 'if', is based on love, then we're less than that clanging gong at Delphi. We are simply a collection of random atoms travelling chronologically together for a while, the song of the universe slowly dying within us.

Love, as Paul rightly observed, outlasts everything.

And once Love came to Earth. Christina Rossetti expresses it tenderly:

> **Love came down at Christmas,**
> **Love all lovely, Love Divine,**
> **Love was born at Christmas**
> **Love for plea and gift and sign.**

31.
The universe itself speaks out the same message. The Greek philosopher Plato believed the shape of the universe was a dodecahedron — a solid with twelve pentagonal faces, not unlike a soccer ball with flattened sections and sharper corners — a shape which has the golden ratio as an intrinsic factor. Studies indicate the Plato seems to have been right: goldennumber.net/universe/ (accessed 18 July 2020) Mathematics itself doesn't exclude the golden ratio within its structure. Pick a number, any number. Pick another number, any number. The only restriction on these two numbers is that you can't pick two zeroes. Add your two numbers to make a third number. Add your second number to your third to make a fourth number, and your third and fourth to make a fifth number. If you happened to choose 0 and 1 as your first two numbers, you'll wind up with the Fibonacci series: 0, 1, 1, 2, 3, 5, 8, 13, 21, 34, 55, 89, 144, 233 and so on. Around $^{55}/_{89}$, you're starting to get very close to the golden ratio. However, it doesn't matter what number you choose. Somewhere between the 1st and 13th iteration, you'll find your numbers tending towards 0.618.

32.
Emphases mine.

Realising God's extraordinary fondness for the number 0.618, would we really expect Him *not* to use it when He chose *where* His Son would be born as a human being? Would He miss an opportunity to tell the world yet again that He is both Trinity and Love?

Not a chance.

God is Lord of the smallest detail, the Father who has clothed the lilies of the field and numbered the hairs on our heads. Of course He didn't overlook the location. There are two latitudes on Earth which could be considered 'golden ratio' latitudes. It wouldn't have mattered whether the Star of Bethlehem was a comet, a conjunction of planets, a supernova or just a five-pointed mathematical shape scrawled in the sand.

Personally my view is that's probably exactly what it was — a diagram, left behind by the prophet Daniel, prophesying the coming of his people's Messiah. Remember he was twice appointed chief of the magi before being taken to Persia. Besides a drawing of the pentagram, which is easily committed to memory, you only need one other piece of information to be preserved across half a millennium with all its attendant vicissitudes of rising and falling empires: you need a starting date for the pentagram 'clock'.

You see, for the magi, angles were measures of time. While that may seem strange today, we actually still retain that ancient understanding of angular measure in our subdivision of degrees into minutes and seconds. The issue, for the magi, was not knowing *where* — but *when*. *Where* was easy enough — since line intersections can denote latitude, it's simply a matter of following a specific line of latitude. That might sound difficult to us, but it's kindergarten basic to any ancient navigator.

The big question is: *when* to start following that line of latitude?

Well, the logical answer is 540 years after the starting date. Why 540? Because that's the number of degrees at the heart of a pentagram.[33] If the starting date is the fall of the Babylon, then the magi could expect the prophecy of the Messiah to be fulfilled 540 years later.

Now Daniel was taken to Persia after the fall of Babylon in 539 BC. That would suggest the magi arrived in Bethlehem in 1 AD. *Except...*

...for a complicating factor. Isn't there always one? We can't be sure what *kind* of years the diagram encodes. Are they *ordinary* years or *prophetic* years? Ordinary years are 365.2422 days; but prophetic years are exactly 360 days.[34] Over a period of 540 years, an adjustment of 2831 days or about 7.75 years is needed.

This would put the date of Jesus' birth back to 6 B.C. which would fit far better with the generally accepted date of Herod's death. Now the magi were not only astronomers, they were also astrologers. In 6 B.C. on 17 April,[35] a very rare eclipse of Jupiter by the moon occurred at dawn—meaning that the sun, the earth, the moon and Jupiter were in a straight line. Jupiter was considered the 'king' planet, the moon was associated with births and the eclipse happened in the constellation of Aries, which in Roman astrology[36] was linked to Israel.

Would God confirm any prophecy like this, using a mix of pagan religions? I think He would. When Jesus came, He wasn't above fulfilling traditional folk beliefs about the Messiah.[37] Moreover, the reason pagan beliefs persist is because generally they are aberrations of the truth.

So ultimately, all the magi had to do was follow the golden-ratio-line-of-latitude west until they reached Judea. This would not have been hard: all they needed to do was make a *gnomon*[38] with a fixed position. As they travelled, they simply needed to stay 'on station'. If they'd had a modern GPS tracking device, they would never have made the mistake of going those few kilometres out of their way to Jerusalem. Not that they can be blamed for going a little off-track. It isn't possible to cross the Jordan River, or climb

33.
Actually, the logical answer is 540 days, not years. However, in the book of Daniel, 1 week is specified as being equivalent to 7 years; therefore, since this means 1 day = 1 year, we can transform 540 days to 540 years.

34.
Corresponding to 360 degrees in a circle.

35.
Michael Molnar, who advocated this date, points out that Matthew's gospel uses a technical term from Greek astrology when saying the star 'rose in the east': it means that a planet rises at dawn, just before the sun. The word 'stood over' is also a technical term, meaning that the planet has appeared to stop moving and is about to enter retrograde motion. This would have happened for Jupiter on 19 December 6 B.C. (theconversation.com/can-astronomy-explain-the-biblical-star-of-bethlehem-35126, accessed 19 July 2020) I have been unable to discover whether Molnar's date is quoted for the Julian calendar (which would have been current at the time) or the Gregorian calendar. This creates a possible discrepancy of 10 or 11 days difference in the dates. Assuming the Gregorian calendar is the correct one, then 17 April 6 B.C. translates to 20 Nisan 3754.

out of the rift valley, just anywhere. The main road west naturally took them to Jerusalem.

But had they been able to ford the stream wherever they liked, they could have simply kept on going right on the exact golden ratio latitude — and wouldn't have stopped until they reached the northern outskirts of a little town just ten kilometres south of Jerusalem called …

…Bethlehem.

Yes, Bethlehem in Judea. The town sometimes called 'the Navel of the Earth'.

Bethlehem is so exquisitely sited that its very location spells out what is written in the very heart of God's mathematical signature: He is Love, He is Trinity, He is Resurrection and Life.

It's at times like this I feel lost for words and have to fall back on an inadequate comment like: "Wow! Isn't that just stunning?" God's geography of grace is not a mystery at all but part of the same astonishing beautiful principle of design He used to create the universe itself.

The word 'mystery' is derived from a word for *silence*. The 'mystery of the Trinity' has been thought of as incomprehensible for far too long. In the days when mathematics, poetry, art and theology were married, the 'Divine Proportion' was known to be God's sign and was known to say He is both Unity and Trinity. However for the last few centuries since those subjects have been divorced, the 'mystery of the Trinity' has been an uncrackable, unfathomable code, constantly said to be beyond our limited human understanding.

Yet the Mystery is simply a silence—a silence which, like the morning stars, is continually singing.

36.
Both Greek and Roman astrology would have been known to the magi who were mathematically adept astronomers as well as diviners and fortune-tellers.

37.
For example, there was a widespread belief that the Messiah would be able to cast out demons. Jesus was the first to do this. There was another belief that there would be a royal messiah called 'the son of David' and a war messiah called the 'son of Joseph' and a priestly messiah after the order of Melchizedek. The gospel of John repeated refers to Jesus as the 'son of Joseph', suggestive of John's intent to present Jesus as the war messiah who would die for the people.

38.
The *gnomon* was a precursor to the astrolabe, which was used to determine latitude by measuring the angle between the horizon and Polaris, also called the North Star, the Pole Star, or Stella Maris (*Star of the Sea*). The *gnomon* and Arabian *kamel* (or *kamal*) was used on land, while the quadrant or astrolabe was used at sea. At that time, the pole would have been about halfway between the stars Thuban and Polaris. They, along with Kochab and Pherkad, two stars in Ursa Minor which are called the 'Guardians of the Pole', would have circled the celestial pole each night. In the twenty-first century, the two outer stars of the Big Dipper can be used as a navigational aid to find the celestial pole; in the first century, Kochab and Pherkad would have given a better indication.

Figure 1

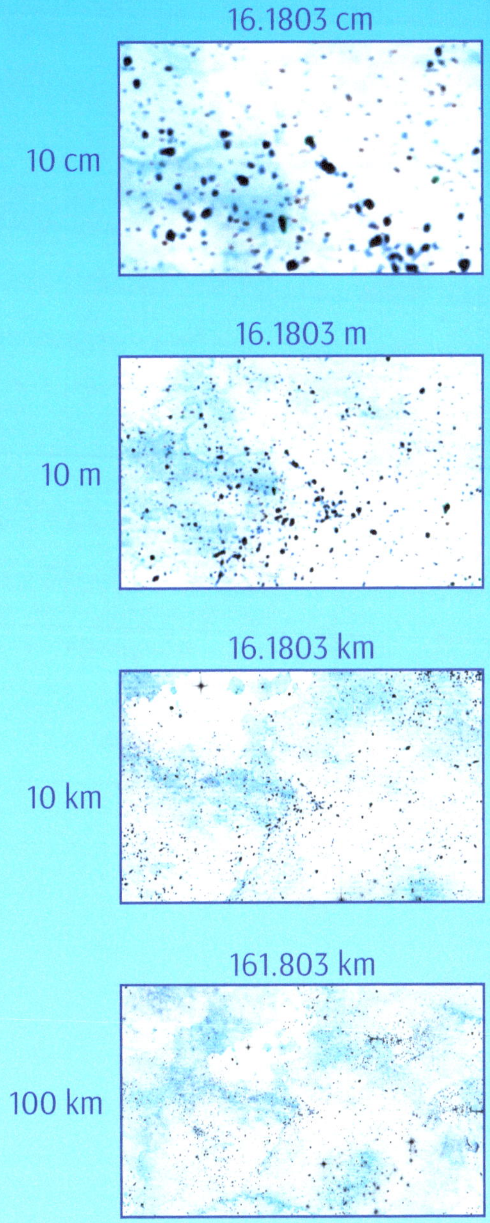

16.1803 cm
10 cm

16.1803 m
10 m

16.1803 km
10 km

161.803 km
100 km

Figure 2
31.71747°

Figure 3
latitude
31.71747°
5419.5 km*
10839 km*

* using the official NASA
radius of 6371 km

Figure 4
BETHLEHEM

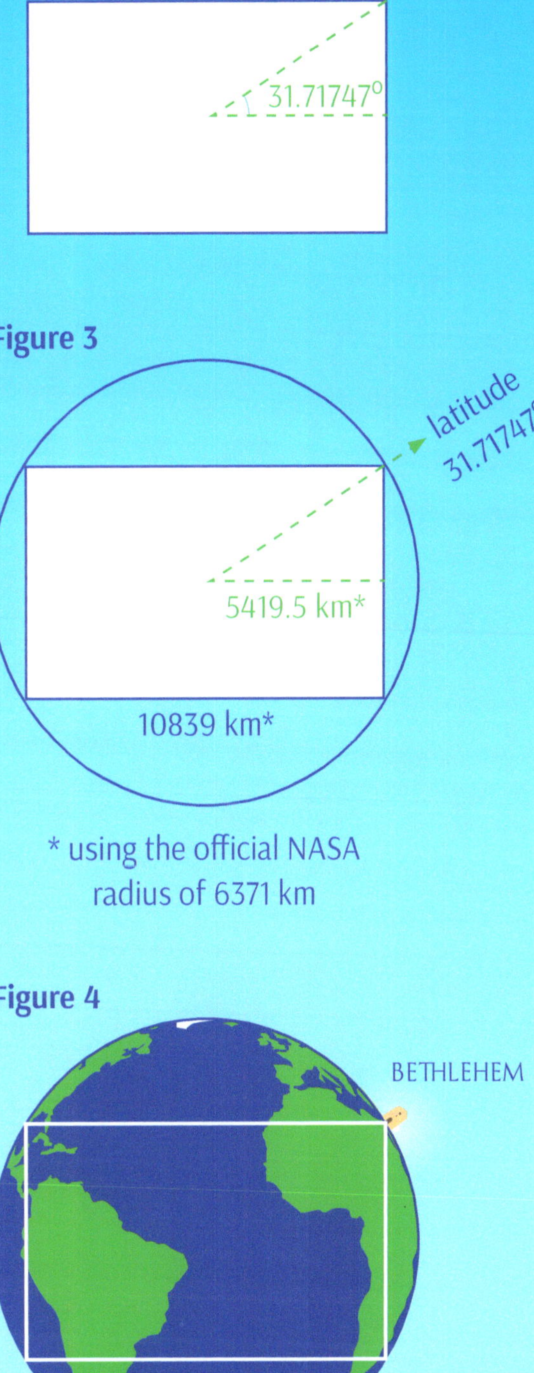

Bethlehem
Jericho
Egypt

He counts the stars
and calls them all by name.

Psalm 147:4 NLT

Micah 5:2 NLT

But you, O Bethlehem Ephrathah, are only a small village
among all the people of Judah. Yet a ruler of Israel, whose origins
are in the distant past, will come from you on My behalf.

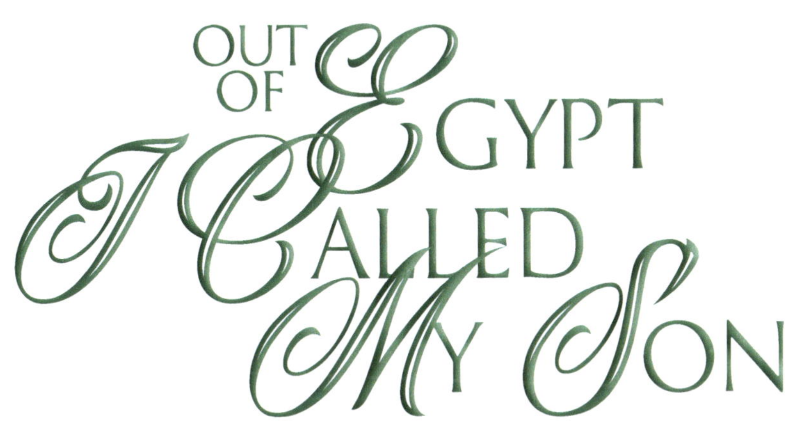

The Lord of armies has blessed, saying,
  "Blessed is Egypt My people, and Assyria the
  work of My hands, and Israel My inheritance."

Isaiah 19:25 NASB

My mother's nose, it's said, changed the world. My father's mind certainly did. He tussled the calendar into a new shape and enforced it across the wide expanse of empire. Not that it was the empire then. And not that it was as vast as it is now. And not that his mind didn't have its own tussles—ones that I share.

Panolepsy—that was his strange weakness. A peculiar thing that a high priest of Jupiter should be possessed by a satyr, the rustic goat-demon Pan of the Greeks, but there was no denying it. The sudden seizures, the jerking fits, the loss of consciousness and tongue-biting were too frequent to hide in his youth. But such was his strength of will that he gained greater control over the demon as he grew older. He would never have risen to the heights he did otherwise.

As a child, I was fearful of the curse he had passed on to me. But, these last few years, I realised it saved my life.

My mother had decided that my future prospects with the Senate would be immeasurably enhanced by a cure. But she didn't want to broadcast the news unless it was a done deal. So, with just one of her Celtic bodyguards as escort, I was quietly sent off with a gift for the god. Payment for my release from the wild one's possession.

Taranis and I sailed up the coast from Alexandria to Dor and there joined the Via Maris, *the Way of the Sea*, travelling up through Meggido to mother's estate at Panias in the foothills of Mount Hermon. We posed as a travelling scribe and his apprentice though, truth be told, Taranis could barely scratch his own name. I think he enjoyed playing the 'master' and making me run errands in the local taverns. I was glad to. The opportunity to gain more than basic fluency in Aramaic was too good to pass up. I even pocketed a few half-shekels in Capernaum, translating a bill of goods for a Parthian trader into Latin.

Taranis thought my glow of pleasure at earning my first pay was absolutely hilarious. But he wouldn't let me keep it. Bad luck, he said. It took me an entire morning to think up a culturally acceptable reason for giving it away. We were passing a priest on the road as we headed north and I stopped him. 'Bikkurim,' I blurted out and pressed the coins into his hands. He looked at me so strangely I wondered if I'd got the word for *first fruits* wrong.

Taranis, with an appalled look, grabbed hold of me and hustled me on. And once we were well out into the wilderness, with no one around, he berated me for making myself memorable. 'If Pan does not accept the gift,' he explained to me, 'we *never* went to Panias. *Never.* You understand, falcon-child?'

I nodded. I understood all right.

As we got closer to Panias, we began to see more and more pilgrims—most on foot, but occasionally there was a donkey or small train of camels. The only time Taranis insisted I cover my face was when we overtook a pair of gilded chariots, each four-in-hand, leading a procession of Nubian slaves wearing peacock-plumed headbands. The Nubians were carrying a silk-covered palanquin. The bells on the heavily laden camels accompanying them tinkled with every sway. The armed guard at the rear and sides looked more decorative than protective. I realised my assessment of them was correct when I saw Taranis throw a contemptuous glance over his shoulder.

It was the palanquin that made us decide to pass the Paneion complex without making any enquiries about a cure. We went straight to mother's estate, thinking we would stay there, safe and hidden, for a few days. We'd wait until the dignitary — whoever he or she was — had come and gone. My nose, Taranis insisted, was a dead giveaway to my identity. No point in taking risks.

We were still there a week later when a messenger arrived from Alexandria. The scroll was terse. It was from my mother, her last words of advice to a beloved son. 'How did she die?' I asked the envoy, holding back both my tears and my fears.

'The rumour is poison.' He saw my sudden scowl and went on. 'It's said by her own hand. She would not be led in a triumph through Rome.'

I nodded and produced my most vacant, dreamy smile. 'Rome? Yes! That's it! I will appeal to the Senate.' I sent the messenger off immediately, back to Alexandria. I had to snarl at Taranis who clearly intended to dispose of the man before he'd even left the estate. 'No!' I snapped, relieved he'd so quickly chosen sides. 'If he's a traitor — which I doubt — he's going to send my enemies in the wrong direction.'

Taranis' grin was almost feral. He nodded his approval. Within the hour we were heading south. We dismissed the possibility of attending the shrine and paying the piper a bribe to release me from Pan's frenzy. The risk was simply too great. I had little doubt my

cousin had sent assassins to follow the messenger but hopefully he was already leading them astray.

The moon was almost full, the celestial river shimmering with stars. We went overland, using the constellations as a guide. Taranis was impressed. 'Sailors and magi,' he said. 'I thought they were the only ones who could navigate by the fires of heaven.'

I'd left our options open. Depending on the way the political breeze was blowing, we could make our way back to Egypt, head east through the desert to Babylon or take ship from Elath to India. Problem was, no matter what choice we ultimately made, we'd have to pass through Herod's territory. And Herod had long ago thrown in his lot with my cousin.

A week into our journey south, again disguised as scribe and apprentice, we reached Jericho. The trip down the length of the Jordan valley had been uneventful. We'd gone by the trade route through Scythopolis, picking up occasional jobs as we went. I translated a shipping manifest for a spice trader from Persian to Aramaic, I checked a bill of sale for a Greek who wanted to buy a shop specialising in Egyptian cotton, and I read a love letter for an illiterate soldier. 'How many languages do you know, falcon-child?' Taranis asked.

'Not as many as my mother does.' I felt a sudden choking around my throat. '*Did*,' I corrected. And then the date palms by the roadside began to spin. I'd held myself together for an entire week, staved off the hunt of Pan as he tried to drive me into unreasoning panic, and I was desperate, desperate, desperate to maintain control. But, in alternating flashes of light and shadow, I lost myself and fell once more into his convulsing embrace.

I woke in darkness, thirsty and alone. *Stay still*, I told my soul. *Orient yourself*. I listened. A snore somewhere beyond the wall, the distant cry of a hunting falcon. I sniffed. Wine, close by. But wafting in on a cool breeze was the heavy aroma of balsam. It was so strong I knew there was only one place on earth I could possibly be: Jericho. Jericho, renowned the world over for its divine fragrances and luscious dates. And I remembered. 'Taranis,' I whispered. There was no reply. 'Where are you?'

I lay waiting until dawn came. When I arose and opened the door, I discovered I was in an inn. And that I'd been there for five days. My return to consciousness seemed to be a cause for celebration: the innkeeper had been promised a bonus if I was alive and well when my 'master' returned. No one had any idea where Taranis was or when he'd be back. I sipped water and nibbled at a fig, careful not to eat or drink too much at once, and thought about the situation. Technically, I probably owned Jericho. Centuries ago, it had been the private estate of Alexander the Great and, of the many gifts my mother had received in her lifetime, it was one of her favourites.

I was still thinking about the situation six days later. I'd walked the circuit of the town, once each day, listening to conversation, trying to pick up news, wondering what had happened to Taranis. In the evenings I returned to the inn, sometimes earning a few denarii for reading or writing or translating a parchment or tablet. As I set out on the seventh morning, a long-bearded priest barred my way. 'I've been watching you, young man.'

I was terrified.

'Are you intending to walk around the city seven times today, not just once?' He held up a ram's horn. 'I've brought my shofar. High time this evil place fell again.'

By the end of the day I'd made a friend of an eccentric Levite who had shared with me not just the long, tangled history of Jericho but also that of Judea. But I also made what, in retrospect, was a fortunate mistake. On discovering I was an orphan, there was no dissuading him. Eleazar took me home and insisted I move into a tiny back room. 'It's too dangerous for a pretty boy like you at that inn. The Name, blessed be He, has protected you thus far. But let us not presume He will continue with such miracles.' He was a widower and lonely, and he loved my company. He was also such a watchful guardian it was impossible to leave.

It was six months before Taranis turned up. He was in uniform, his oiled breastplate glistening in the sunlight. Shocked, I watched him stride into the inn and then come out, clearly pale and frantic. His astonishment when he finally spotted me was evident. 'Are you a ghost, falcon-child?'

'Where've you been?' I demanded, ignoring his question.

'Jerusalem,' he answered. 'I'd only just got you to the inn when a couple of old friends marched in. They recognised me. Your mother's bodyguard is now in Herod's employ. I had no choice but to leave you. This is the first chance I've had to come back. I thought I was coming back to pay a debt, not to find you.' A wide smile started to curve across his face. 'I thought you'd been taken. You know your cousin says you're dead.'

It was the longest speech I'd ever heard from Taranis. 'How convenient for him then that, if I did turn up, I'd be an imposter.'

Taranis flicked me a shekel. 'Good translation,' he growled, as he spun me to face the wall and stalked off with a pair of blue-cloaked soldiers. Celts. I recognised the tattooing.

It was another six months before I saw him again. This time he sought me out at Eleazar's. He had to wait. My business as a scribe and interpreter was thriving. 'I've kept it safe,' he said, surreptitiously handing me a leather pouch. 'The gift for the god.'

I almost didn't know what to say. Tears sparked in my eyes as it dawned on me how loyal Taranis was. He was forfeiting a future for himself of freedom and luxury. 'Thank you.' My half-choked whisper was husky with emotion.

Eleazar's eyes were growing dim but his mind was sharper than ever. 'A Celt from Galatia,' he said. 'Recognise the accent. Fiercest mercenaries there are. Utterly ruthless. So when's he coming back?'

I shrugged. 'He didn't say.'

In fact, it was a year before Taranis turned up again. It was difficult, he said, to get leave — he'd been promoted to the garrison at Bethlehem. I rolled my eyes. 'You're minding sheep?'

'Worse,' he reported. 'Water.' He sighed. 'Herod is planning to expand the Temple. Make it more glorious than Solomon's ever was. So, water for sacrifices. Lots of it. I'm keeping watch on the builders of the new aqueduct from Bethlehem.' He smiled and I noticed he'd lost a tooth. 'It's always about water. Don't you know that, falcon-child?'

I thought of the Nile and the years without flood. And I remembered a story Eleazar had told about David's mighty men and the Philistine-held well at Bethlehem. Taranis was right: the ordinary lives of farmers and the extraordinary deeds of heroes both revolved around water.

That night I asked Eleazar about Bethlehem. 'It's the birthplace of Messiah,' he said.

I was confused. 'I thought that was Egypt.' Hadn't Moses, the greatest of all Jewish deliverers, been born in my homeland? Moses, Prince of Egypt, torn by conflicting loyalties, handicapped by diffidence, was my source of hope. If he could overcome stuttering speech, I could overcome stuttering limbs.

'Egypt!' Eleazar glared at me. 'Riddle me this, child of the Nile. What is it in the air of the Black Land that befuddles the sons of Israel so they can't leave the golden calf behind?'

Child of the Nile? He'd never called me that before. How did he know? And how did he know the Egyptian word for our own land? But, more than that, how did he know about the gift for the god? I'd secreted it carefully and knew its hiding place hadn't been disturbed. Did he know who I was?

'Jeroboam,' Eleazar snapped. 'Goes down to Egypt, comes back, foments an insurrection and sets up a golden calf. The sons of Jacob go down to Egypt, come back, rebel against the Name and set up a golden calf.'

I'd never had an episode since I'd come to Jericho. But now I felt the sweeping dizziness. 'I'm not a son of Israel,' I managed to get out.

'The prophet Isaiah who witnessed the majesty of the Name in His throneroom reported that the King of glory said this about the nations: *"Blessed be Egypt My people, Assyria My handiwork, and Israel My inheritance."* The Name has claimed you for His own. Do not despise His choosing.'

I took a deep breath. He wasn't going to throw me out. The dizziness subsided. 'It's not a calf,' I said. 'It's a goat.'

'A golden *goat*?!' Eleazar clapped his hand over his mouth. He began to laugh uncontrollably. It was contagious. After a few seconds, I saw the funny side too.

I brought it out of its hiding place and showed it to him. In the guttering lamplight, it was hard to tell what it was supposed to be. Goat, sheep, deer, calf—it could have been any of them. The maker had fashioned an ambiguous form. 'What should I do with it?'

Eleazar was still rocking with laughter. 'Do you know why Moses ground the golden calf up and make the people drink a concoction of gold powder and water?'

He was silent as I thought. A minute went by. Two. 'Covenant,' I said at last. 'He was compelling the people to acknowledge their covenantal oneness with the gods of the Black Land. After all, you are what you eat.'

'It's one thing to take a son out of Egypt,' Eleazar said. 'It's entirely another to take Egypt out of the son.' Concern for me edged every word. 'Jeroboam was a good man, chosen by the Name to bring reform to the tyranny that marked Solomon's later years—but, through those golden calves he set up, Jeroboam became forever renowned as the one who caused Israel to sin.' He locked eyes with me. 'And Aaron was a good man, chosen by the Name to help Moses give birth to a nation. But he too caused Israel to sin. And Moses himself, after forty years of talking to the Name just like a friend, he still struck that rock. You know what that means, don't you?'

I nodded. I understood the customs of hospitality of this land. 'He refused covenant.' I took a deep breath. 'Did your God offer him another name, as He did for Abram and Jacob?'

'You know the story. If you think about it, you will know what was offered and how often it was offered. But he never accepted it. He always kept the name Pharaoh's daughter had given him. As I said, it's one thing to take a son out of Egypt and entirely another to take Egypt out of the son.'

I lay awake all that night and, as dawn came, I broke the golden goat apart. Symbolic of breaking covenant with Pan. I put the pieces in the leather pouch and hid it again. I wasn't yet ready to choose the Hebrew god but I renounced all ties with the wild hunter. Whatever happened in the future, I wasn't going back to Panias.

The years went by. If the political situation had destabilised, I might have gone to Rome and made my appeal to the Senate. But my cousin forged an increasingly stable empire. He might have been a rapacious dictator but his iron rule brought peace. As it did, trade flourished and my business prospered.

Still the years went by. Taranis dropped by when he could but the time between visits became longer and longer. I accused him of having a girl and, to my disbelief, he blushed. It turned out he'd married—quietly, of course, because Herod's troops were to have only one priority in life.

One Rosh Hashanah, I surprised Eleazar with a gift. I paid the annual hire on a hall so he could teach students. The shock and the joy and his sobbing tears brought me undone. That night, I took a mallet and smashed the pieces of the goat into ever-smaller lumps. But still I hesitated about a final commitment to Eleazar's God. It's one thing, as he said, to take a son out of Egypt and entirely another to take Egypt out of the son.

And then… then into the steady, rhythmic march of months and seasons came a disturbance. Some locals found two strange, grey-bearded men on camels wandering around near the ford of the Jordan. They thought the men were traders and, early one morning, they brought them to me, hoping I'd be able to understand their heavily accented Aramaic. I switched to Greek but, although they clearly understood, their replies sounded even more atrocious. I tried Persian. And instantly we were communicating. 'We are searching,' they said, 'for the king of kings.'

I felt the blood drain out of my face. A whoosh of stars crossed my vision. I felt the panic rising and the fluctuating roil of light and dark. 'We have seen his natal-star rise in the east,' they went on, oblivious to my trembling, 'and have come to worship the one born King of the Jews.'

The dizziness cleared, the shaking stopped. *King of the Jews.* I sucked in a relieved breath. *Of the Jews.* 'Are you magi?' I guessed.

They nodded.

'Food and drink for you and your camels first. Directions, second.'

As I arranged for them to be fed and watered at the inn, I did some quick thinking. My father had been Flamen Dialis, high priest of Jupiter, and I knew enough astrology — especially about the king-planet — to converse knowledgably on the topic. 'To rise in the east' was a technical term for a dawn ascension. Could the natal-star be Jupiter? It was, after all, the sign for Judea in the star lore of the Greeks.

I sent for Eleazar. I needed urgent help: one thing was sure, if these men were here for the advent of the Messiah, they needed to be concealed. If Herod found out about them, they wouldn't last an hour.

Fortunately I was wrong. Still I underestimated Herod's spies.

Eleazar had just arrived as the magi sat down to a repast of goat, beans and barley. I ordered another jug of wine and, at that moment, the door smashed open. Herod's guard strode in. I knew better than to say a word. Eleazar and I were scooped up with the magi, loaded onto a couple of chariots and, the camels bleating piteously at being dragged along behind us, driven up the steep road from Jericho to Jerusalem.

It was a lightning move. How Herod had found out I couldn't even begin to imagine. Actually, I didn't want to imagine. Someone in Jericho—a friend, a neighbour—was an informer. Before the morning was out, we were hustled into Herod's presence.

He was everything I did not expect. His gracious welcome included precious oils for our heads and cool water to wipe the dust from our feet. A genial and smiling host, he poured the finest of spiced wines for us, sipping his cup first to demonstrate it was safe. He spoke Latin and got no response from the magi. He spoke Greek and was rewarded with a ghastly, incomprehensible mangling of faintly recognisable syllables. He inclined his head towards me. 'Interpreter,' he said. 'Welcome these foreigners to the Kingdom of Judea in their own language.'

I did so. I suspected Herod had the rudiments to do it himself so I was careful to keep to the basic diplomatic formula. I felt so relaxed so suddenly that I was instantly concerned. *What was in that wine to loosen tongues?* I had to get Eleazar, at least, out of there. But the inquisition of the magi was already underway. *Who were they? Where had they come from? How long had they taken to get here? What route had they taken? Had they been encountered trouble or delays? Why had they come? What made them think a king was born? How long ago did the star first appear? Did their own ruler know they had come? Was their visit official? When were they expected to report back?*

Always smiling, always amiable, Herod was relentless in his questioning of these bowed, decrepit men. The inadequacy of my training in Persian soon became apparent. But whenever it did, the magi simply repeated, 'We saw his natal-star rise in the east and have come to worship the One born King of the Jews.'

Finally Herod said, 'It is a mystery of the gods. I will consult with the chief priests.'

'It is no mystery,' Eleazar muttered. 'For this is what the prophet has written: *"But you, Bethlehem, in the land of Judah, are by no means least among the rulers of Judah, for out of you will come a ruler who will be the shepherd of My people Israel."'*

Herod smiled and left us alone to finish the meal. The old men babbled to themselves in a barbarian language I didn't know. But sure that the walls had ears, I was careful to speak of inconsequential things until Herod returned. 'Bethlehem, indeed,' he confirmed. 'Escort our guests where they wish to go. But do it secretly, so that the people are not inflamed with rumour and speculation. And tell our guests this: "Go and search carefully for the Child, and when you find Him, report to me, so that I too may go and worship Him."'

We were taken out the back of the palace, reunited with the camels and sent off. I was glad to escape with my skin intact. I'd never been to Bethlehem and neither had Eleazar but, remembering what Taranis had told me, I scouted around for an aqueduct leading towards the Temple. It was a simple matter of following it back south. But with three ancient men to guide, I found our progress to be interminably slow.

Eleazar was troubled. 'I don't know whether we will find the Messiah or not but we can never go back,' he said to me. 'I saw the way Herod looked at you. Puzzled, as if he couldn't remember where he'd met you before. He will eventually work it out.'

'He's *never* met me before,' I pointed out.

'He knew your father!' Eleazar almost shouted. 'And your mother tried to seduce him.'

I couldn't help but stare. 'How long have you known who I am?'

He didn't answer. 'I knew something was wrong when I awoke this morning. I knew I would lose you today.'

'Don't say that, father,' I said. I had never called him 'father' before, but it came out naturally, unbidden.

'So I brought your smashed goat.' From the folds of his tallit, Eleazar pulled out the leather pouch. And, as he handed it to me, we both started laughing. I hugged him and linked his arm in mine and, together, we led the magi south, following the aqueduct. I tried to hurry them all so we would reach Bethlehem by sundown, but their individual resistance was fierce, their combined resistance more so. I should have realised the magi were actually waiting for nightfall. As soon as the stars were out, they threw off their dusty cloaks and pulled out charts and equipment. And by the sudden vigour of their actions, I realised these were not ancient greybeards at all, but men in the prime of their youth. They were younger than me. 'What is the date?' one asked me.

I wondered if they knew my father's calendar. But it seems they did. They were thrilled. 'Tonight,' the other said, 'the king-star will stand still before it goes into retrograde motion. The timing is perfect.'

'Now to find the exact place,' the first said. He held up a strange kamal, one without knots in the string. I realised it would only ever allow them to navigate by one singular latitude. But that restriction is clearly what they wanted. He held the kamal up to make the sighting. 'Kochab and Pherkad guard the north.'

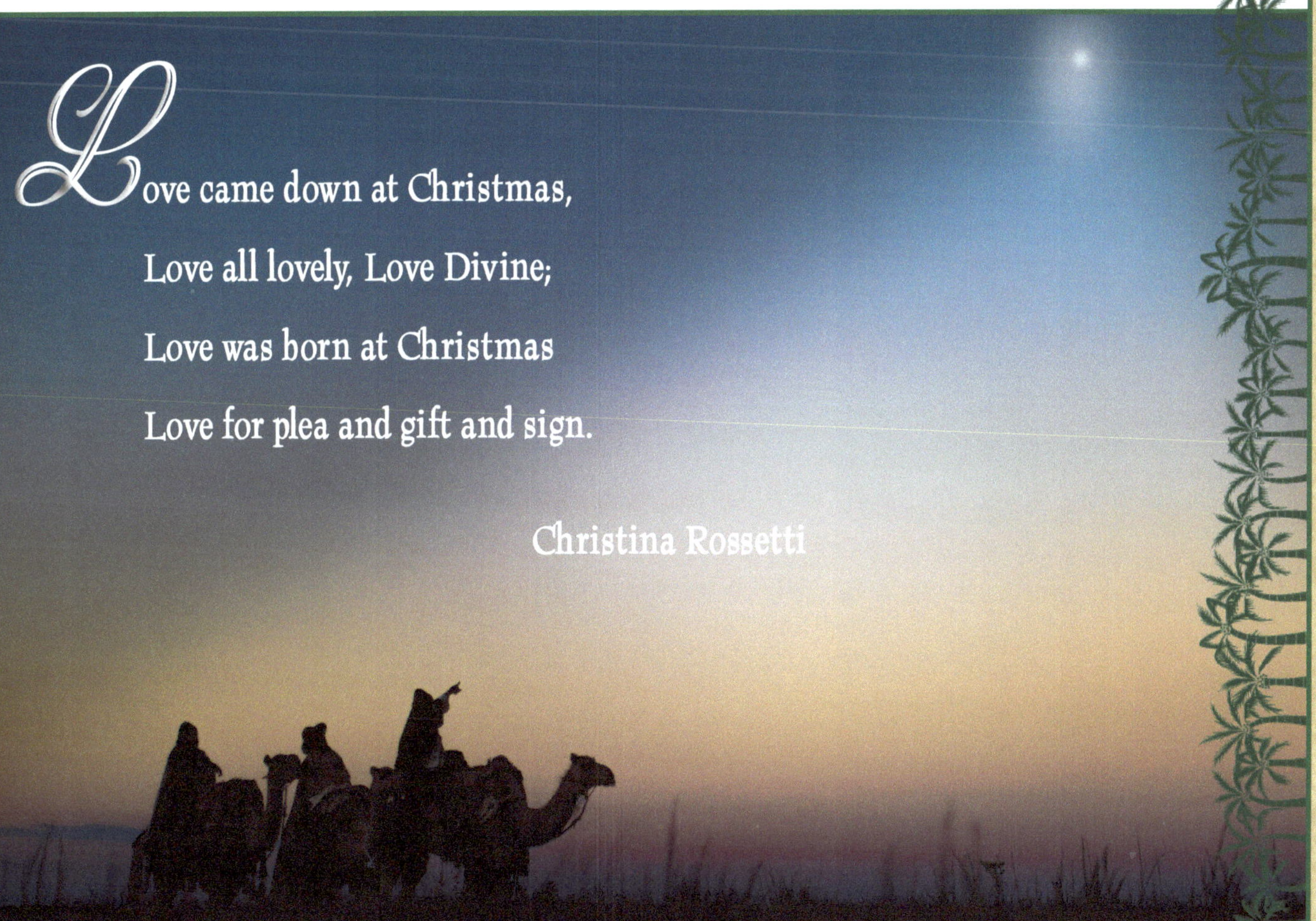

'The two star-calves,' I said. In the Black Land, these were two of the markers of the pole that showed a deceased Pharaoh the gateway to the afterlife. *Calves*, I thought. And my mind turned to *golden* calves… and then to covenant.

I was still thinking how much more difficult it was to take Egypt out of a son than it was to take a son out of Egypt when Eleazar pinched my arm. 'Be careful what you show them.' His whisper was in Hebrew — to ensure the magi didn't understand. 'We must not make Hezekiah's mistake.'

I frowned in puzzlement.

'The seat of the magi is Babylon,' he said. 'When the envoys came from Babylon in the time of Hezekiah, he showed them everything. Yet he did not show them enough.'

'What was enough?' I asked.

'He did not introduce them to the God of Israel. Instead he introduced them to his treasures — to his gold and his spices.' Eleazar straightened. 'The time has come again. The Name, blessed be He, has given us an opportunity to repair our estate. Let us honour the hour.'

I was about to tell Eleazar I was the wrong person for any such nation-mending when the magi whooped.

'There!' they both shouted, as they began running. The kamal and the charts were flung aside, the camels loped after them and Eleazar and I brought up the rear. I watched the magi regain their dignity as they approached a small courtyard. They walked solemnly the last few steps into a circle of firelight and knelt before an infant. Frankincense and myrrh were their offerings.

A man was there with the young mother. They both looked startled at the unexpected intrusion and the strange accents of their visitors. Eleazar moved forward. 'What is the child's name?' he asked.

'Yeshua,' the man answered. 'God saves.'

'These men have travelled afar, a long way and a long time,' Eleazar said. 'They have come from the distant east to see the King of the Jews.'

The man nodded. He didn't seem surprised at the designation. 'Did an angel direct them?'

Eleazar shook his head. 'A star.' He hesitated. 'May we bless the young King?'

The young mother handed him the babe. And so the blessings began. Eleazar and the magi, rocking the child back and forth, singing lullabies and prayers, whispering blessings and thanksgivings.

I kept back, afraid of the flicker kindling in my heart. But I knew. Oh, I knew what I had to do. The call of covenant was upon me. More urgent than Pan's pipes had ever been. I sidled around to the man and handed him my leather pouch. 'Herod knows about the boy,' I whispered. 'Leave soon.'

The man stared at the medallion attached to the thong of the pouch. Beneath its grimy exterior it was pure gold. 'These are hieroglyphics,' he murmured. 'What do they say?'

I hadn't expected that question. I almost didn't answer. 'They say: *beloved of his father, beloved of his mother, god, son of god, king of kings*. Most assuredly, it belongs to the Child. This, my heart tells me is deep and true.'

The man frowned at me and I could see his mind working out the titles. And then the realisation and the recognition. 'Caesarion,' he whispered. 'Son of Julius Caesar and Cleopatra of Egypt, last of the Pharaohs. *You* would pay *us* homage?'

I nodded. 'It is only fitting.' I took another risk. 'There is a man in Bethlehem who will help you. His name is Taranis, a Celt who serves in Herod's Guard, but he is loyal and honourable. You can trust him.'

As the magi slept that night, dreaming fitfully, I stayed up with Eleazar. 'I'm going east,' I said as we sat side by side in front of the dying fire. 'With the magi. They won't go back to Herod. They're too astute. But what will you do, father? You can't return to Jericho.'

'I'm thinking a small school,' he admitted. 'Nothing too grand. Somewhere in the Galilee, perhaps. I feel a call to train small boys who aspire to be rabbis.' He laid his head against my shoulder. 'I never wanted to do it before. Because of the hold of Egypt within us.'

He paused. 'But now I realise the Messiah will wrest Egypt out of the sons of Israel. This is not a matter of faith...' He nodded, raising his hand in final blessing. '...but of observation. For I have already seen it happen in the son of my heart.'

Historical Background

In the previous volumes of this series, the stories have been narrative retellings of episodes in Scripture from the perspective of a bystander. The story above is different: it's a genre change into historical fiction. Ever since I read that Cleopatra's Guard was taken into the employ of Herod the Great, I've longed to write a story featuring one of these Celtic mercenaries.

So let me outline the historical facts from which the imaginative story above has been woven: Cleopatra did indeed employ a band of warriors from Celtic Galatia who, on her death, went to work for her rival, King Herod. They subsequently played a prominent role in his funeral. The gifts of land Cleopatra received from her Roman lovers, Julius Caesar and Mark Antony, included the city of Jericho as well the region around the town of Panias, later to become Caesarea Philippi. She was also given joint rights with Herod to the bitumen deposits of the Dead Sea. Many of the desert fortresses Herod built — including Masada — are thought to be a direct result of his paranoia about Cleopatra's territorial ambitions.

Herod's impressive building programme included the expansion and restoration of the Second Temple. The daily sacrifices required huge volumes of water for cleansing and purification. However, the springs of Jerusalem were unable to supply the vast quantity needed, especially during festival time. An aqueduct system that included storage pools sluiced water in from Bethlehem. Besides these resources, a large number of personnel were needed for Temple services. It is estimated that, in the time of Jesus, ten thousand Levites lived down the valley from Jerusalem in the city famous for its palms and perfume — Jericho.

It is believed Cleopatra spoke nine languages. She claimed to have had a son by Julius Caesar and, while this was never publicly acknowledged, it was never denied either. The son was named Ptolemy XV Philopator Philometor Caesar, that is, Ptolemy XV *beloved of his father, beloved of his mother, Caesar*, and he was commonly called Caesarion, *little Caesar*. When he was thirteen years old was proclaimed to be *god, son of god*, and *King of Kings*—thus announcing that he was Caesar's true son and heir. This provocative declaration was a direct threat to Octavian (later to become Caesar Augustus) who, as Julius Caesar's adopted son, had staked his own claim to power.

Caesarion is believed to have suffered from epilepsy, as did Julius Caesar. This condition was then known as 'panolepsy' and was considered to be the result of possession by the demi-god Pan, the guardian of flocks and herds. Pan was a half-human, half-goat hybrid regarded as the protector of Greece because he had allegedly driven the Persian armies into panic—that state of terror named after him. One of the most famous shrines to Pan in the ancient world was located near a cave called 'the Gates of Hell' at Panias. Both animal and human sacrifice was practised there. Visitors to this shrine often sought a cure from epilepsy by making a gift to Pan.

Jesus visited this place—by then renamed Caesarea Philippi—and it was there that Simon declared Him to be the Messiah. He returned to the same location after the Transfiguration, there encountering the father of the boy who suffered from fits and who would often throw himself into the fire. The disciples had been unable to help the boy. Jesus roundly condemns the father, clearly indicating that his purpose in coming to the shrine was to make a sacrifice to Pan for the release of his son.

Caesarion is believed to have been killed by order of Octavian but the circumstances are unclear. In this fictional account, I have made use of the vagueness of his death to suggest he survived in hiding.

Because, indulgent as this story is, it was also irresistible to write of a real-life historical personage with the titles *beloved of his father, beloved of his mother, god, son of god*, and *King of Kings* who pays homage to Jesus of Nazareth. It might not have happened as I recounted it, but on that great day when every knee will bow before the Lord of all who was born in Bethlehem of Judea, it will happen.

$\mathcal{P}$ROPHETIC $\mathcal{B}$ACKGROUND

On occasions it's seemed to me that the gospel and epistle writers played fast and vague with prophecy. Sometimes it looks like they've stretched it a loooooooooooong way to cause it fit the life of Jesus and at other times it seems like they've shaved the sides of a square peg to force it into a round hole.

A particularly annoying niggle for me in the past has been these words of Jeremiah quoted by Matthew in reference to the massacre of the children of Bethlehem: *'A voice is heard in Ramah, weeping and great mourning, Rachel weeping for her children and refusing to be comforted, because they are no more.'*

That doesn't make sense.

The children of Bethlehem were not descended from Rachel—their ancestral mother was Leah.

The children of Bethlehem were not from the tribe of Benjamin or Joseph—their ancestral father was Judah.

The children of Bethlehem were not from Ramah, a town on the boundary between the territory of Benjamin and Ephraim.

In fact, Rachel wasn't from Ramah—so why mention it? Rachel was originally buried near Bethlehem, so Ramah just serves to confuse the matter. Perhaps it's mentioned because both clans that border it—Benjamin and Ephraim—are descended from Rachel… but there's still an apparent large degree of inexactitude in this prophecy. Surely Jeremiah should have mentioned Bethlehem?

Now the problem is not Jeremiah's or Matthew's. If you're like me, you look at the surface and seek for a mention of the obvious. It's therefore so easy to miss the ancient tragedy they were trying to evoke with their words — and which Jeremiah was prophesying is not over, but would happen again. And again.

Way back in the time of the Judges, a feud started between the people of Bethlehem in Judah and the people of Gibeah in Benjamin. Behind it was the death of a woman of Bethlehem in the town of Gibeah, and the subsequent genocide of the tribe of Benjamin: 98% of the male population was wiped out and all of their women were massacred.

Reason enough for Rachel to be *weeping for her children... because they are no more*. The conflict went on intermittently for generations and, by the time of the first few kings, it involved both Saul — whose hometown was Gibeah — and David — whose hometown was Bethlehem. A careful look at the names in Saul's family tree reveals an intriguing element: there are many names that belong to the rulers and deities of the kingdom of Edom. Furthermore Saul had a trusted high official — his chief herdsman, Doeg the Edomite. When Saul's own royal guards were unwilling to kill the innocent priests of Nob for unknowingly helping David escape, it was Doeg who executed them.

Here's another reason for Rachel to be weeping for her children — they'd allied themselves with those who were willing to slay the innocent.

Fast forward over a thousand years to another high official under a foreign ruler — Herod the Great. Herod was a client king under the Roman emperor. He was also an Idumean — that is, an Edomite.

David and Jesus both escaped the wrath of the reigning king, but the innocents around them did not. Just as Doeg the Edomite massacred the priests of Nob, so Herod the Idumean ordered the massacre of the boys of Bethlehem.

Both Doeg and Herod have names with similar overtones. Although Herod is said to mean *son of a hero*, to a Hebrew speaker the name would have sounded like *coward* or *fearful*. That's the root of the name Doeg, too — *fearful* or *anxious*.

The tears of Rachel in Jeremiah's prophecy refer, in my view, to jealousy and feuding that ends in the massacre of innocents—in whatever era it happens. Even our own. Fast forward nearly two thousand years from the time of Jesus' birth to the mid-nineteenth century. Once again, jealousy and feuding in Bethlehem led to the death of many innocents: a conflict over the keys to the Church of the Nativity in Bethlehem led to the Crimean War.

Even today, that conflict in the Church there still simmers. Perhaps we should not be surprised. Bethlehem is traditionally translated *house of bread*, but since the words for *bread* and *warfare* are identical in ancient Hebrew, it could also be rendered *house of battle*.

The healing that Jesus accomplished in other locations does not seem to have happened in Bethlehem because the pattern keeps repeating itself, even into our own century. Yet, having said that, mystery abounds because later in His life, Jesus stepped into this complex tapestry of death and destruction and reversed it. He showed us how the healing of history could restore all things, even life itself!

Rachel's tears begin with her second son, whom she named Ben-oni, *son of my sorrow*. She died giving birth to him and his father quickly renamed him Benjamin, *son of my right hand*. The first king of Israel, Saul, came from the tribe of Benjamin. And although Saul lost both the kingship and any hope of a dynasty through his disobedience to God, he was still a great man who in the early part of his reign healed many deep rifts in the national psyche. True, he did not end well–but it's tough to find a king who did.

It's incredibly easy to overlook the honour that Jesus paid to Saul. In receiving the news that Lazarus was ill and leaving Bethany-beyond-the-Jordan to go to Bethany outside of Jerusalem, Jesus walked—seemingly point-to-point, if we examine the geographical clues—the very same route that the bones of Saul were carried when David had them exhumed and re-interred just outside Jerusalem. Saul's name is related to Sheol, *the underworld*, so it is no coincidence that Jesus, in walking this path, prepared to assail the gates of the underworld in raising Lazarus from the dead. Moreover, when Jesus was anointed king—on the evening before He rode into Jerusalem on a donkey, the ceremony did not occur in the City of David but in Bethany, *house of sorrow*. Not only does the name hark back to Ben-oni, *son of my sorrow*, it was also in the territory of Benjamin—Saul's ancestral homeland.

We underestimate the destructive spiritual power of dishonouring our leaders—even those who are deceased. The honour that Jesus showed to the first king of Israel is exceptional; the King of kings, the sovereign Lord of all creation, paid His respects to a flawed earthly regent. This was a precursor to bringing Lazarus forth from the tomb—and seems mysteriously connected to the covenant Saul made with the underworld on the night before he died in battle.

One persistent image of the underworld for the Hebrews was 'the Black Land': Egypt. Joseph the dreamer, the son of Rachel and Jacob, was sold into slavery by his brothers. They'd planned to kill him but instead they got rid of him to some Ishmaelite traders—who were travelling from Gilead to Egypt with balm, myrrh and spices.

Another Joseph, also a dreamer, also went down to Egypt with balm and myrrh, barely escaping a death threat to his foster-son, Jesus. (Frankincense is also called *olibanum* which in turn is known as *balm*.)

The first Joseph was given the name 'Zaphenath Paneah' by Pharaoh, thought—amongst a range of meanings—to denote *Saviour of the World* for his wise preparation towards seven years of famine. This name is prophetic of Jesus of Nazareth, the Saviour of the World who redeemed mankind from the consequences of sin.

Joseph was able to say to his brothers: '*You meant evil against me, but God meant it for good, to bring it about that many people should be kept alive, as they are today.*' (Genesis 50:20 ESV) In the same way, although Herod meant evil against the little family of Jesus, Mary and Joseph, their flight into Egypt was meant for good that, by preserving the life of the baby who was to become the Kinsman-Redeemer of all who believe in Him, vastly more lives would be saved.

Yet there's an obvious difference between those 'things' that accompanied the two Josephs to Egypt. In both cases, myrrh and balm—or frankincense—went down. But gold only went with the second Joseph—and that seems to be a reversal of kinds. Gold is famously associated with the 'despoiling' of the Egyptians by the Hebrews when they were freed from slavery—they asked for jewelry and were given it. And, although some of that gold was later used in the furniture of the Tabernacle, it was much more memorably used to create the golden calf.

The golden calf is usually seen as rebellion against God. Yes, there is that—but the motivation at the heart of its construction is not, in my view, a spontaneous decision to insult God but implacable and total unforgiveness. They hated Pharaoh, loathed the works he'd forced them to build, were furious at his broken promises. In essence: they had not forgiven Egypt for enslaving them.

When we fail to forgive others we do one of two things—condemn ourselves to repeat the very same sins we so passionately hate or condemn ourselves to repeatedly draw to ourselves the kind of people who will commit the sins we so passionately hate.

So, for the Israelite people, their unforgiveness condemned them to repeat the things they hated. The cities and monuments of ancient Egypt were very precisely aligned to particular astronomical markers. Among the most significant of these are the stars, Kochab and Pherkad, the 'two calves' who were seen as *guardians of the pole*. They were guides, indicating the celestial pathway for a deceased Pharaoh to safely pass into the afterlife. In those days, it wasn't possible to use Polaris as a waypost because it was not situated near the pole at that stage of history.

In a later age, Kochab and Pherkad could have been utilised by the magi to find the latitude during their journey to the west. So perhaps, in the visitation of the magi, we see a reversal of the golden calf and the star lore associated with it: since, guided by a star, the magi offered gold in worship to the 'King of the Jews'.[1]

The golden calf was not just a symbol of Egypt, it was a symbol of the alignment of its cities and monuments, it was a symbol of the hard-hearted deceased Pharaoh and it became a symbol of both apostasy and broken promises. Egypt was the land of broken promises. But the Hebrew people, in failing to forgive, failed to release themselves from spiritual bondage—even while their physical bondage was removed—and therefore perpetuated the cycle of broken promises.

Centuries went by and more golden calves were set up. Jeroboam, one of Solomon's taskmasters, was prophesied to tear apart the kingdom because Solomon's heart had hardened against God. Forced to flee for his life, he went down to Egypt and did not return until Solomon had passed away. He then led the rebellion against Solomon's son, Rehoboam, and set up a rival kingdom as well as worship centres for his new subjects—one at Bethel and one at Dan. Both of them had

1.
 The 'King of the Jews' is a title that bookends the Gospel of Matthew. It is found in the second chapter, and also the second last chapter — and is always a designation of identity recognised by foreign rulers. At the beginning of the Gospel, it is the magi; at the end of the Gospel, it is the Roman governor, Pontius Pilate.

golden calves. Again we see the same elements in the background to the erection of these idols: Egyptian influence, unforgiveness for slavery, a hard-hearted ruler, broken promises to God.

It's one thing to take a man out of Egypt, but entirely another to take Egypt out of the man. As Jeroboam did not return from Egypt until after the death of Solomon, so Joseph the foster-father of Jesus, did not return from Egypt until after Herod's death.

Hosea had announced God's once-and-future declaration, *'Out of Egypt, I called My Son,'*[2] and Matthew proclaimed the fulfillment of this prophecy had occurred with Jesus.[3] However, this isn't a simple statement about a journey to the land of the Nile and back again: it's also once-and-future. Since Egypt was, for the Hebrews, a symbol of the underworld, it looked forward to an even more momentous event — the coming forth from the 'Black Land' of the tomb as Jesus burst the chains of our slavery to sin.

The Lord of Hosts will bless them, saying, 'Blessed be Egypt My people, Assyria My handiwork, and Israel My inheritance.'[4]

Still let us learn the lesson of the golden calves: unforgiveness keeps us bound. When others break their promises to us, we do well to forgive them — lest we become promise-breakers ourselves.

Because the Prince of Peace and Promise-keeper, Jesus of Nazareth, wants to lead us in triumph out of the Black Land and into the inheritance He won for us.

2. Hosea 11:1 ESV
3. Matthew 2:15 ESV
4. Isaiah 19:25 BSB

2. Hosea 11:1 ESV
3. Matthew 2:15 ESV
4. Isaiah 19:25 BSB

TRADITION

When it comes to the birth of Jesus, there are often more traditions than facts. Many of the uncertainties about Christmas arise because, until the fourth century or so, the celebration of birthdays wasn't a normal part of any ancient society. The dates for a tragedy or for a death were considered important and remembered for millennia, but births were not part of cultural consciousness. However with the rise of astrology a time came when they did start to be important, and naturally Christians wanted to know about Jesus' birthday so it could become part of a calendar of celebration. Unfortunately by this time, centuries had passed, and only fragments of knowledge were preserved. Personally, I think one of these tiny pieces of information handed down through the generations was that Jesus was born around about New Year — but, in calculating the most likely date, it seems a vital fact was overlooked. The New Year of the Roman Empire bears no resemblance whatsoever to the Jewish New Year.

Nevertheless, despite the fact that 'Christmas' should almost certainly be commemorated in September, God has shown surprising grace towards tradition. He hasn't condemned it just because it is tradition — and oftentimes, He has fulfilled it anyway. Such instances of satisfying tradition include the widespread belief in the first century that the Messiah could be identified by His ability to cast out demons. No one is recorded in the Scriptures as performing deliverance until Jesus.

Another tradition that Jesus fulfilled was the understanding that there would be a war messiah called 'son of Joseph' as well as a royal messiah called 'son of David'. Now the expectation was that the war messiah would come from the tribe of Joseph and certainly it seems no one anticipated they would be the same person, but it is clear that there was indeed a surprising realisation of this tradition.

A further tradition that Jesus made use of was the feast of Hanukkah, *the festival of lights*. This is not one of the God-appointed feasts but rather a man-made observance of a military victory. Yet Jesus used the symbolism of Hanukkah to heal a man born blind and proclaim Himself the 'Light of the World'.

And possibly another tradition that He fulfilled — though this one is uncertain — is the belief that the Messiah would be born at Migdal Eder, *the tower of the flock* — a watchtower in Bethlehem used by the shepherds guarding the perfect and unblemished lambs before they were sent up

to Jerusalem for the Temple sacrifices. Yet another tradition is the name of the magi and their number and their attire: allegedly three of them, said to be called Balthasar, Caspar and Melchior and frequently pictured in conical hats topped with five-pointed stars. Curiously, the first name is a form of Belteshazzar, the name given to the prophet Daniel in Babylon. And the five-pointed star, as I have pointed out, encodes both the location of Bethlehem and the time period to start looking for the King who created the mathematics of the star.

It seems to me that, if our traditions point to Jesus, God seems more than willing to show us grace. So let us ensure that is always and ever the case.

Discussion Questions:

(1) The very first verse of Genesis encodes mathematics that points to the latitude of Bethlehem. Does this give you a deeper surety that Jesus is not only the Word Made Flesh but the Creator Himself?

(2) What special things in your life cause you to remember the message hidden in every created object: God is love, God is Trinity, God is Resurrection and Life?

(3) The first part of this book has one basic theme: *if everything in the universe is signed with a divine seal that Love will come to Bethlehem, then it doesn't really matter whether the Star the magi followed was a supernova, a comet, a conjunction or occlusion of planets or even a mathematical diagram.* Do you agree or disagree with this?

(4) What traditions can you think of that surround Christmas that are entirely secular in character? What traditions actually do point to Jesus as the 'reason for the season'?

(5) Are there parts of your heart that are still harbouring grudges over broken promises? Is 'unforgiveness' a golden idol that you need to ask Jesus to smash for you?

(6) If If Jesus can heal the history of nations, He can heal our personal history. What do you need to ask Him to walk through in your life to bring restoration to yourself, your family and your community?

(7) How has God called you to show that He is Love, Trinity, Resurrection and Life to others?

PRAYER

Heavenly Father,

Hallowed be Your name. I dare to take hold of the tassels on the hem of Love's cloak and I ask Jesus of Nazareth, King of kings, to purify my prayer as He presents it to You. Through His intercession, may my words be made holy, may my words be made humble, may my words be empowered, may my words be a spring of blessing, may my words be a blossom of healing, may my words usher in Your kiss of love wherever I go, may my words always honour You.

'*What can I give Him, poor as I am?*' asked Christina Rossetti. And she answered *my heart*. O yes, Heavenly Father, I surrender my heart. I give it as an unholy and inadequate gift to You, because there are parts of my heart that are conflicted and resist You at every turn. They remember the broken promises of earthly authorities — parents, guardians, teachers, bosses — and they transfer the blame to You. Those wounded parts are unforgiving, Lord, and even when they want to forgive, which is far from always, they can't. They are stuck in grief and bondage.

Father, grant me the empowering grace to speak words of forgiveness and have them settle in my heart. Break apart my idols, Lord, because I can't smash them myself — but I give You permission to do everything necessary to pluck them from my life.

Unite my heart, O Lord, to reverence Your name — and to know You as Love, as Trinity, as Resurrection and Life. Unite me to You, Lord, through the Blood of Jesus, in the Name of Jesus, over the Cornerstone of Jesus, through the Supper of Jesus and in His Peace.

Call me out of the underworld, Lord, and call the underworld out of me.

In Jesus' Name. Amen.

In the bleak midwinter, frosty wind made moan,
Earth stood hard as iron, water like a stone;
Snow had fallen, snow on snow, snow on snow,
In the bleak midwinter, long ago.

Our God, Heaven cannot hold Him, nor earth sustain;
Heaven and earth shall flee away when He comes to reign.
In the bleak midwinter a stable place sufficed
The Lord God Almighty, Jesus Christ

Enough for Him, whom cherubim, worship night and day,
reastful of milk, and a mangerful of hay;
Enough for Him, whom angels fall before,
The ox and ass and camel which adore.

Angels and archangels may have gathered there,
Cherubim and seraphim thronged the air;
But His mother only, in her maiden bliss,
Worshipped the beloved with a kiss.

What can I give Him, poor as I am?
If I were a shepherd, I would bring a lamb;
If I were a Wise Man, I would do my part;
Yet what I can I give Him: give my heart.

Christina Rossetti

Acknowledgments & Attributions

Photo and Arts Credits

Cover and page 4 – Ondřej Prosický / Dreamstime | Description: Nero Glasswing; closeup of transparent glasswing butterfly

Page 5 – fotofritz / Canstock | Description: Rainbow Valley Central Australia

Page 7 – David M Sacerdote / Dreamstime | Description: Blue Poppie

Page 8 – PsychoShadow / Canstock | Description: Silhouette of a lonely giraffe against a foggy, orange sunset.

Page 10 – m-gucci / istockphoto | Description: Space mosaic of comet, Earth, Moon and stars.

Page 13 – benedek / istockphoto | Description: Landscape photo of the distant Gosses Bluff in the southern Northern Territory; Grafoo / Dreamstime | Description: Pine cone. Staff by Beckon Creative

Page 14 – Komprach Nitiborisutsakul / Dreamstime | Description: Pineapple; Denise Johnson / Unsplash | Description: Ready for liftoff; Amirali Mirhashemian / Unsplash | Description: Brown snail

Page 15 – luckydog / Canstock | Description: Calla spiral; Vaclav Volrab / Dreamstime | Description: ladybird on the grass

Page 17 – turnervisual / istockphoto | Description: A new fern leaf springs open; Christokruger / Dreamstime | Description: Lanner Falcon

Page 18 – Hunterston Brooch / Wikimedia Commons

Page 20 – Eugene_Sim / Canstock | Description: Nautilus; magann / Canstock | Description: image of an anemone's flower; page 99 in paperback by Tolkien, *Sir Gawain & the Green Knight/Pearl/Sir Orfeo*, George Allen & Unwin (Publishers) Ltd 1979

Page 23 – Anyaivanova / Dreamstime | Description: Parthenon temple at sunset; Lucila De Avila Castilho / Dreamstime | Description: Flowers hanging

Page 24 – Piotr Paczyński / Dreamstime | Description: Leonardo da Vinci's proportions of the human body; Mauro77photo / Dreamstime | Description: Red leaf studio shot; Anne Hamilton | Description: Found feather

Page 27 – Isselee / Dreamstime | Description: Closeup of panther chameleon; Wikipedia | Description: Crab Nebula; graph of Crab Nebula pulses; Kamchatka / Canstock | Lily of the Valley

Page 30 – Eivaisla / Dreamstime | Description: Apple element; Yong Hian Lim / Dreamstime | Description: Cross-section of a papaya; Veerachon Sithiprai / Dreamstime | Description: Yellow star flower

Page 32 – Jessamine / Dreamstime | Description: Muiredach's High Cross at Monasterboice, Ireland; Ralph (Ravi) Kayden / Unsplash | Description: Green four leave clovers; PeterHermesFurian / iStock | Description: Gray colored Platonic solids 3D and black wireframe models. Regular convex polyhedrons with same number of identical faces meeting at each vertex. English labeled illustrion over white. Vector; Ondřej Prosický / Dreamstime | Description: Grey parrot with crest. Probosciger aterrimus, talon in the bill, New Guinea

Page 34 – Loflo69 / Dreamstime | Description: Blue borage; Pink badger / Canstock | Description: Anemone hepatica; Andipantz / istockphoto | Description: Dried Queen Anne's Lace flower; Ying Feng Johansson / Dreamstime | Description: Anemone hepatica; Friendly dragon / Canstock | Description: Closeup of single thistle flower

Page 37 – John Theodor / istockphoto | Description: Olive trees in Shepherds Field with view of Bethlehem at sunset

Page 38 – Sergii Kolesnyk / Dreamstime | Description: Pyramid in sand dust

Page 40 – Jacek_Sopotnicki / istockphoto | Description: East side of the Galilee Sea

Page 41 – odyphoto / iStock | Description: Architectural antiquities in natural reservation of Hermon river (Banyas) - Cult center of the god Pan, north of Israel

Page 42 – lorado / istockphoto | Description: Celtic warrior

Page 43 – Alessandro La Becca / Unsplash | Description: brown eagle on gray wooden fence in tilt shift photography

Page 44 – tashka2000 / Canstock | Description: Bottle of myrrh

Page 46 – anyka / canva | Description: apostle; ayvengo / istockphoto | Description: gold metal bull; peterfactors / Dreamstime | Description: Stone Window

Page 47 – Waleed_Hammoudeh / istockphoto | Description: Sunset of the Pyramids and the Sphinx in Cairo

Page 49 – kavram / Canstockphoto | Description: Transparent spring morning in mountains of samaria. velvety hills are shined by the morning sun

Page 51 – Pearl / Lightstock | Description: wisemen traveling on camels

Page 52 – photographer / istockphoto | remains of palace in Jericho

Page 54 – Artokoloro/ Alamy | Bethlehem and surroundings

Page 55 – Valdemaras D / Unsplash | Description: Jericho

Page 63 – badahos / Canstockphoto | Description: Mountain views in in israel, masada

Page 67 – Danil63 / Dreamstime | Description: Follow the star

Design, including endpapers and iconography: Beckon Creative | beckoncreative.biz

Bible Versions

Scripture quotations marked AMP are taken from the Amplified Version of the Bible Copyright © 2015 by The Lockman Foundation, La Habra, CA 90631. All rights reserved. www.lockman.org

Scripture quotations marked BSB are taken from the The Holy Bible, Berean Study Bible, BSB Copyright ©2016 by Bible Hub Used by Permission. All Rights Reserved Worldwide.

Scripture quotations marked ESV are taken from the ESV® Bible (The Holy Bible, English Standard Version®), copyright © 2001 by Crossway, a publishing ministry of Good News Publishers. Used by permission. All rights reserved.

Scripture quotations marked ISV are taken from the Holy Bible: International Standard Version®. Copyright © 1996-forever by The ISV Foundation. ALL RIGHTS RESERVED INTERNATIONALLY. Used by permission.

Scripture quotation excerpted from THE JERUSALEM BIBLE, copyright ©1966 by Darton, Longman & Todd, Ltd. and Doubleday, a division of Penguin Random House, Inc. Reprinted by permission.

Scripture quotations marked KJV are taken from the King James Version of the Bible. Public domain.

Scripture quotations marked NAS are taken from the New American Standard Bible®, Copyright © 1960, 1962, 1963, 1968, 1971, 1972, 1973, 1975, 1977, 1995 by The Lockman Foundation. Used by permission. (www.Lockman.org)

Scripture quotations marked NLT are taken from the Holy Bible, New Living Translation, copyright 1996, 2004. Used by permission of Tyndale House Publishers, Inc., Wheaton, Illinois 60189. All rights reserved.

Scripture quotations marked NIV are taken from the Holy Bible, New International Version®, NIV®. Copyright © 1973, 1978, 1984, 2011 by Biblica, Inc.™ Used by permission of Zondervan. All rights reserved worldwide. www.zondervan.com The "NIV" and "New International Version" are trademarks registered in the United States Patent and Trademark Office by Biblica, Inc.™.

Scripture quotations marked RSV are taken from the Revised Standard Version of the Bible, copyright © 1946, 1952, and 1971 the Division of Christian Education of the National Council of the Churches of Christ in the United States of America. Used by permission. All rights reserved.

Scripture quotations marked TLB are taken from The Living Bible copyright © 1971 by Tyndale House Foundation. Used by permission of Tyndale House Publishers Inc., Carol Stream, Illinois 60188. All rights reserved.

Scripture quotations marked TPT are taken from The Passion Translation®, Isaiah: The Vision copyright © 2018 by Passion & Fire Ministries, Inc Used by permission. All rights reserved. ThePassionTranslation.com

Published by Armour Books

P. O. Box 492, Corinda QLD 4075 AUSTRALIA

ISBN: 978-1-925380-38-5

A catalogue record for this book is available from the National Library of Australia

There are two symbols, bread and money;

and there are two mysteries,

the eucharistic mystery of bread

and the Satanic mystery of money.

We are faced with the great task:

to overcome the rule of money and

to establish in its place the rule of bread.

Nikolai Berdyaev